KERB

24

Journal of Landscape Architecture

2016

••

Kerb is published annually by Actar Publishers.

ISBN 978-1-922129-49-9
ISSN 1324-8049

Library of Congress Control Number:
2016948657

Each edition of **Kerb** is produced by a new student editorial team.

••

••

Art Direction
Sean Hogan – Trampoline Design.

Graphic Design
A collaboration between the editors and Sean Hogan - Trampoline Design.
trampoline.net.au

Acknowledgments
The editors would like to thank everyone involved in the production of the journal for their generous assistance and support during the process of this publication.

••

For orders, advertising and all other enquires contact:
ActarD Inc.

New York
355 Lexington Avenue, 8th Floor
New York, NY 10017
Phone: +1 212 966 2207
Fax: +1 212 966 2214
Email: salesnewyork@actar-d.com

Barcelona
Roca i Batlle 2
08023 Barcelona
Phone: +34 933 282 183
Email: eurosales@actar-d.com

www.actar-d.com

ACTAR

LANDSCAPE ARCHITECTURE
RMIT UNIVERSITY

RMIT
UNIVERSITY

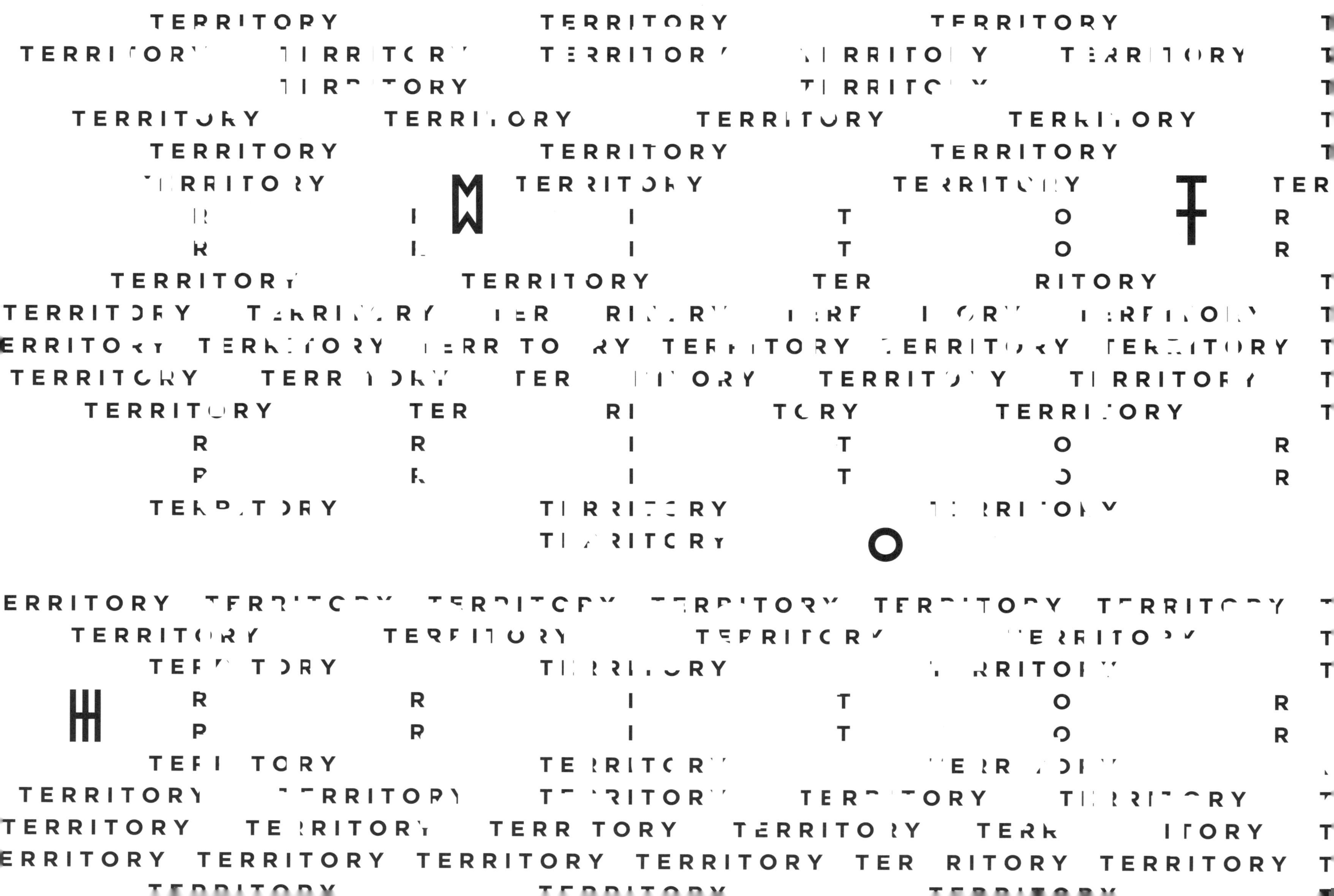
TERRITORY

TENSION

OBSERVATION

TERRITORY

LOUELLA EXTON
EMMA GROOT
MILLICENT GUNNER
HAYDEN MATTHYS
KIM MORTE

Territorial and spatial conditioners, the systems concerned with the organisation and order of space, operate at a range of scales. On the small scale, the cohesion of space is driven by a compositional and aesthetic framework, tended to through time. On the territorial scale, spatial arrangement is impacted by environmental, political, jurisdictional, economic and cultural processes. This macro set of operations completely abandons micro scale interactive methods of spatial conditioning. It downgrades the potential to actively shape the landscape, degrading it to simply a passive material on which the larger operations play out. Globalised and economically focused agendas of the territorial are often undertaken with little consideration to local and culturally rich landscapes. Yet the overwhelming nature imposed by the vastness of the territorial makes matters of the compositional seem redundant by comparison **(Tension)**. Documentation and commentary surface such tensions and drive a need for action **(Observation)**. Landscape holds the potential to mediate across the two scales through active and inclusive spatial conditioning employing methods of composition which are sensitive to but not ruled by the operations of territory **(Mediation)**. In doing so, landscape balances the growing complexity of the global[1] (where borders are open for certain international flows- namely powerful international corporations - and closed for others - migrants and refugees) with the detail and locality of the micro scale. Landscape re-establishes connectivity between the micro and the macro across time, not to privilege one scale over another in conditioning space, but rather to act as the moderator between territory and terrain **(Expansion)**.

Tension

Matters of territory manifest in the material landscape or terrain, often as border crossings or walls, to secure territorial limits between neighbouring states. Further projections of power and ownership are enforced through maps. The point of transition, thought to have a nominally zero width, through adjoining territories is reinforced, and in a way personified, by these techniques.

This exaggeration of the transition point, as marked by the boundary or line, is limiting in terms of understanding and accuracy.[2]

This ongoing process, in which the edge of the field is progressively redefined, is undeniably conditioned by the force of time. To try to preserve the edge or outer limit is an omission of this integral and inescapable force. Instead of imposing inhibitive limitations, there is a potential to engage creatively with expressions of territorial identity and the acceptance of the progression of time. We argue that a static and blanket response to the large scale is counterproductive to the complexity inherent in relationships between territories.

For Le Roy, minimal to no intervention is necessary for a superior system of complex organisation.[3]

We propose a middle ground in which the continuum of time is an essential consideration, and chaos and inhibitive regulation is moderated.

Ambitions to rigidly define territory become more problematic when social and cultural groups are ignored due to institutional opposition to legality or legitimacy. Often excluded from official

1. This complexity is apparent in that changes to any one system operating within this territorial scale has ramifications for other systems within the vast global network. See: *A Conversation with Saskia Sassen* and Schmid, Brenner and Topalovic's *Cartographies of Planetary Urbanisation*, published in Kerb24.

2. A Conversation with Stuart Elden: *Approaching Territory.* Kerb24

3. Roy, Louis G. le, Vollaard, Piet., Boukema, Esther, & Veìlez McIntyre, Philippe. (2002). Louis G. Le Roy: Natuur, cultuur, fusie = nature, culture, fusion. Rotterdam: NAi Uitgevers.

city maps, informal settlements that commonly emerge on a city's periphery become invisible to mechanisms of urban regulation. In the case of the city of Lima, a redefinition of a divided territory is called for. Researcher Claudia Bode suggests 'that by working to include these newly defined territories into the overall 'image' of the city, it would knit Lima to itself to form a more coherent whole.' Mapping here could transition from the problematic to the antidotal, and begin to cultivate a system of fairness across a territorial distribution.

Observation

Similarly within observation lies the power of recording and representing. The changing and shifting of territory, and the need to understand this, initiates visual representations. There exists a constant conversation between the landscape, how we interpret it and the platform on which it is represented. It is this back and forth process of translation that sees the abstraction of information. Combined with the knowledge of other sources, landscape as mediator has the potential to deeply unpack territory.

The borrowing of information sees elements of overlay, collation, and intersection arise to form a visual documentation. Importantly, diagrams and mappings record the larger activity of processes. The inclusion of narrative in this recording captures the more ephemeral and atmospheric qualities at the scale of the individual. The challenge lies in how well a visual language can broaden our understanding of concerns across scales. 'A Cartographic and Political Enquiry on Borders and Climate Change' by Italain Limes, works with the complexity of landscape observation through dealing with its dynamic features through interactive modes of representation. Documenting fluctuating borders, rapidly changing ecologies, and even the migrations of people, challenges the static nature of common cartographic methods.

In the first steps of moderating previously disparate conditions of site, landscape drawings can work to communicate to other parties. However, they are still only a commentary and, in some cases as discussed by David Heymann, drawings are superficial in privileging aesthetic excellence for the purpose of industry. Drawing itself is, arguably, relatively passive. There comes a point where a physical realisation, an active intervention, becomes a true mediation between territory and land.

Mediation

Where initial recordings become the foundations for designed interventions, landscape embraces its unique position in the hierarchy of spatial conditioners. Landscape holds the potential to pose equity across the scales of the territorial with that of the terrain. Just as territorial processes can be revealed through a manifestation in the land, so too are acts of landscape mediation.

Mediation involves the consideration of larger networks, broader relations, and processes of global connectivity. It addresses the inevitable changing and fast paced nature of what can be seen as a living, breathing, uncontrollable presence of territory. This must come without neglecting landscape's inherent ability to work with form and composition through aesthetic and tending frameworks, keeping a rich understanding of the embedded qualities of culture and heritage. The act of considering these polarising concerns leads, in turn, to actions that address tensions between local and global scales of operation.

Landscape is embedded in the layer where the dynamics of territorialisation become spatialised. It can be seen as active in the negotiation between scales of occupation, arbitrating between the larger scale of global networks of economics and industrialisation, and the local scale of the community. As Brent Ryan's work suggests, through changes of occupation new territories emerge or existing territories are reconfigured. Through this reconfiguration, the landscape in which the territories operate is changed, and hence the processes operating within the territory are changed also. Re-imagining previously impacted sites can ignite new occupation and brands of public life.

Expansion

Conditioning engenders a distinction between an active landscape and the processes impacting upon it. Both play a role in the formation of space, with processes embedded in the land through time, intertwining with the territorial to constantly reshape space. It is in this feedback loop between terrain and territory that landscape is found, and mediation occurs across all scales. From the micro moments to the large scale networks, all are constantly made and remade by interacting conditioning processes. It is from this understanding that we push for a view of landscape not as a static outcome, merely to be mapped and built upon, but landscape as an active player in territorial conditioning.

As Brenner, Schmid and Topalovic explore in Cartographies of Planetary Urbanisation, urban regions can be understood as differential nodes of global and regional networks. This orientation sees space as conditioned by networks which link built systems to territorial systems. They are broadening the scope. Territory is more than what is merely observed on the ground.

At its extreme, this conditioning is talked about in conversation with socioeconomic theorist Saskia Sassen. Sassen critiques the new era of systemic logics emerging from the political economy of the 20th Century. She concentrates on destructive forces relating to globalisation and the enlargement of territorial processes which cut across historical, geographical and conceptual boundaries.

'Spatial consequences are treated as accidental by-products of these networks'[4]; yet seeing space as an 'accident' of a greater network of processes limits ones ability to grasp and work with them.

The expanded network of territorial conditioners becomes a problem when it is viewed in isolation and removed from the landscape which it conditions. Landscape is not the by-product of territory - it takes an active role in its shaping.

Conclusion

Landscape is in a constant state of change, characterised in correlation to space, place and time. Through a break from traditional cartographic methods of interpreting landscape as static form, to a more dynamic mode of recording process across landscape and territorial concerns, landscape is able to be observed as an active agent in the formation of space.

The work presented within this edition of Kerb extends our understanding of territory and landscape, from the vast network of processes to the moments experienced in place. By acknowledging and engaging with landscape as a spatial organiser, it then becomes a mediator of processes across all scales of operation.

4. Easterling, K. (2014). Extrastatecraft: The power of infrastructure space.

GLOSSARY OF TERMS

Land:
material, ground plane, canvas, micro scale.

Landscape:
an abstracted view of terrain within a perceivable range, the mediator between scales.

Field:
an invisible barrier or force.

Volume:
the contents of the field, the macro scale, the network of territorial registers, processes, and relations existing through time.

Edge:
the perceivable range of the volume.

Boundary:
the mark of an area's limits.

Border:
the administrative division or demarcation of ownership, or, to be adjacent to.

Barrier:
an obstacle preventing movement .

Conditioning:
to have a significant influence on, or to bring (something) into the desired state for use, or to set prior requirements on (something) before it can occur.

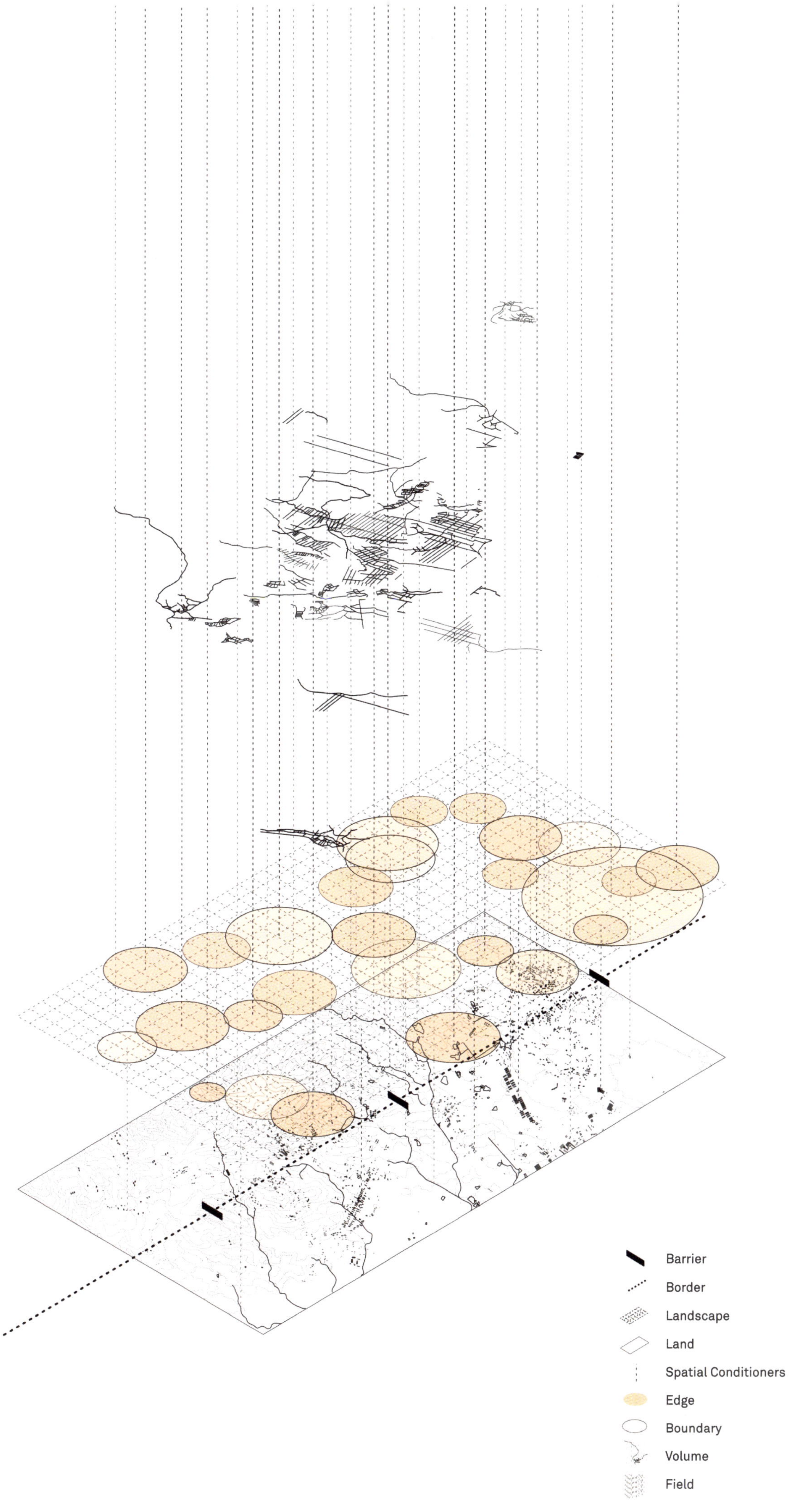
Barrier
Border
Landscape
Land
Spatial Conditioners
Edge
Boundary
Volume
Field

TENSION TENSION TENSION

TEN ION TENSI N TE

TENSI N

ENSI N TEN ION

TEN ION TENSI N TE

E N

TEN ON ENS ON NSI N TE

E N

ENS ON TEI SION TENSI N TEN ION

TENSI N

ENSI N TEI SION ENSI N TEN SION ENSI N TEN ION ENSI

TENSION TENSION TENSION

ENS ON TE

E N

ENS ON TEI SION TENSI N TEN ION

TENSI N

ENSION TENSION ENSION TENSION ENSION TENSION ENSI

TENSION

TENSION TENSION

ENS ON TEI SION TENSI N TEN ION

TENSI N

EN T O NS T O IS TI OI SI

TEN ION TENSI N TE

E N

TENSION TENSION TENSION TE

E N

ENS ON TEI SION TENSI N TEN ION

TE ON IS TE

TENSI N

ENSI N TEN ION

TENSION TENSION TENSION

ENS ON TE

E N

TI NSIO T NSI N ENSI N

E N

TENSION TENSION TE

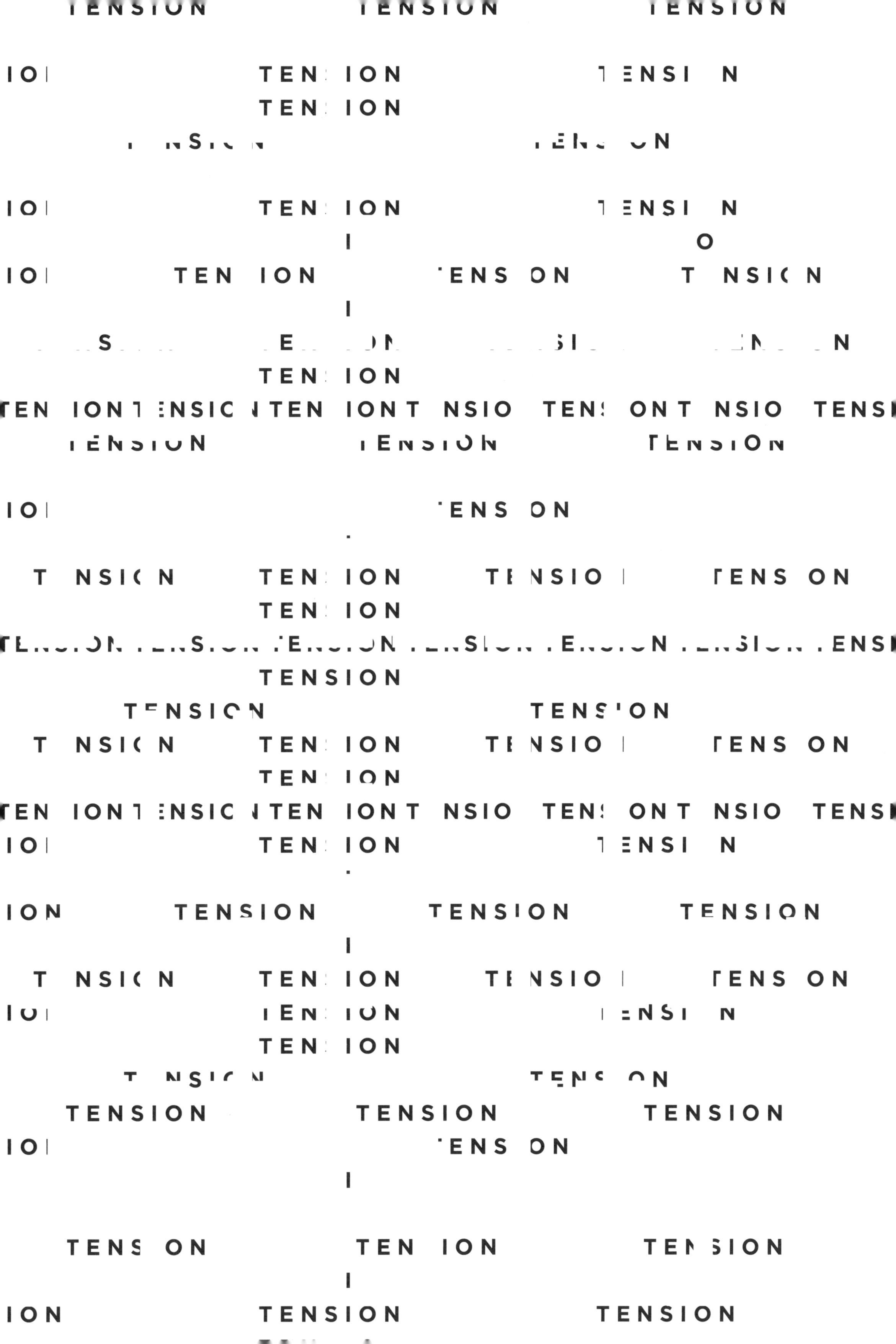
TENSION

Claudia Bode

RE-TERRITORIALISING LIMA : THE ROLE OF THE VISUAL IMAGE

Re-territorialising Lima: the role of the visual image

Lima, a city of 10 million people squeezed into the desert between the Peruvian coast and the Andes, is territorially ruptured at multiple scales - between the center and periphery, within its hilly informal neighborhoods, and between colonial and pre-Hispanic notions of landscape. This essay examines the work of a program called Barrio Mio, which was deployed from 2012 to 2014 to re-scale parts of Lima's peripheral territory, and also explores the role of cartography and other means of visual representation as a tool for urban re-territorialisation.

Invisible City

Lima, Peru, like other large Latin American cities, is marked by differentiation between its flat, formal center and its hilly, informal periphery. These two Limas coexist symbiotically and unevenly, with the highly diverse character of the city's informal areas (the *barriadas* or *pueblos jovenes*) reflecting shifting levels of government involvement over the decades. The 1940s to the 1960s saw a series of Peruvian leaders who invested in the city's quickly growing fringes, allowing for the construction of the innovative PREVI projects as well as other research into social housing.[1, 2] Since the late 1970's, however, state support has been withdrawn in concert with the growth of neo-liberal economic theories[3] replaced in part by the distribution of property titles meant to increase access to the market. This solution reflects the significant influence of Hernando de Soto and others who take a 'legalist' approach to informality in Latin America[4]. The withdrawal of state resources coincided, in the 1980s and 1990s, with mass migration to the city by Peruvians under threat from terrorist groups, as well as with the exhaustion of available flat land and the resulting uncontrolled creep of informal housing into steep and seismically active mountains.[5] Currently, more than 60 per cent of the city lives in conditions of informality, with many of these residents building small houses on steep hillsides, highly vulnerable to a wide range of social and environmental risks including poor education, social exclusion, lack of electricity and water, earthquakes, landslides, and lack of access to credit and banking.[6]
The residents of these informal areas travel long distances to work as domestics, cooks or street vendors in Lima's wealthiest neighborhoods, but in reality there is often very little

Below right:
Typical tourist map of Lima, showing only the central area

Below:
40 PUI zones 9 identified by Barrio Mio including the Huaycan area of Lima, on the periphery.

Above right:
Huaycan area of Lima, on the periphery.

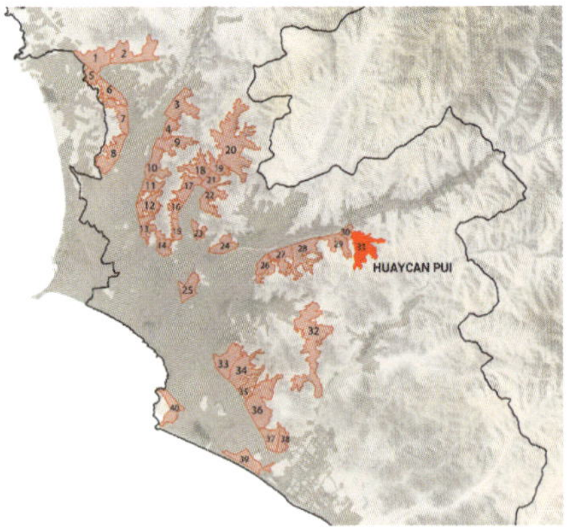

meaningful contact between citizens of these two worlds. The vast majority of the residents of Lima's formal areas have never intentionally travelled into the periphery of the city, which, despite containing most of Lima's population, receives very little attention from the media, the government, or popular culture. The invisibility of Lima's poor periphery is reflected and exacerbated by the city's highly fragmented system of political representation, in which under-scaled political units prevent neighbourhoods from developing coherent visions that can be used as planning tools. Instead, small groups of citizens petition the government for funding for shortsighted proposals (such as a football field) with little to no coordination between neighbours.[7] The result is a patchwork of disconnected projects (if they are built at all) and little real political agency.

As a response to the conditions of poverty, vulnerability and invisibility endemic to Lima's informal settlements, the city inaugurated a program called Barrio Mio ('My Neighborhood') in 2012. The program, which was shut down at the end of 2014 by the current mayor, ostensibly aimed to address the needs of residents of Lima's periphery through participatory planning and urban design workshops, retaining walls and access stairs, and social programs.[8] In reality, the aim of Barrio Mio was to address political fragmentation by bringing together people who lived in contiguous zones (defined by topographical and social boundaries) and building political agency through the creation of unified, neighbourhood-scale urban visions.

Sociologist and spatial theorist Neil Brenner defines re-territorialisation as the 'reconfiguration and re-scaling of forms of territorial organization,' a shifting which re-scales planning decisions and the nuances of power.[9] By re-scaling territorial divisions within the periphery of Lima, the Barrio Mio program would address the persistent political invisibility of a large sector of the city. By working to include these newly defined territories into the overall 'image' of the city, it would knit Lima to itself to form a more coherent whole. As such, the work of Barrio Mio, as well as the research that followed the official end of the program, cannot be separated from its visual representations. Through diagrams, maps, architectural renderings and other images, existing territorial divisions were challenged; at multiple scales, the desired goal was to change not only political divisions but, ultimately, mental representations of

1. Many descriptions of Limas previous projects exist online. For instance, go to www.architecturalpapers.ch/index.php?P=104 for a description of Lima's PREVI projects.

2. Luis Rodriguez Rivero, Interview about Barrio Mio and its Representational Techniques, May 4, 2016.

3. Fernandez-Maldonado. (2007). A. Fifty Years of Barriadas in Lima: Revisiting Turner and de Soto. Rotterdam. p. 15.

4. Alsayyad, N. (2004). Urban Informality as a 'New' Way of Life, in :Urban Informality: Transnational Perspectives from the Middle East, Latin America, and South Asia. Lexington Books, Lanham, MD. p. 13.

5. CONURB (2016). La Cuidad de Las Laderas. Lima, Peru. p. 8.

6. Ibid 5

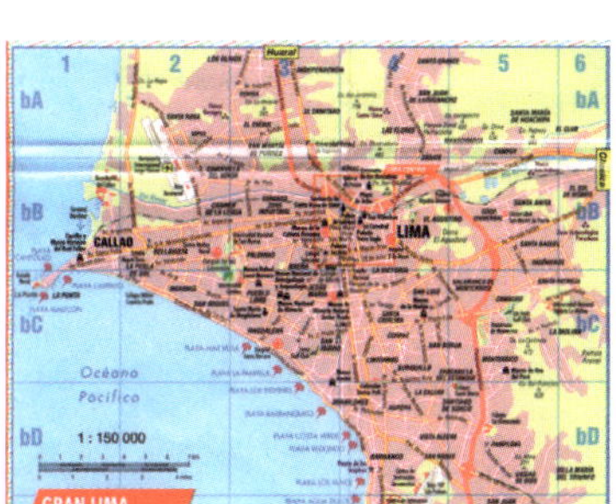

territory. These images are powerful, but their potency is also embedded in the methods with which they are produced (*mappings* vs. maps)[10] the result being that the entire process of creating visual representations of territory can be implicated in the actual creation of new and re-scaled territories.

Rescaling Local Territories

In order to probe the relationships between the representation of territory (which often takes the form of a map) and the territory itself, it is helpful to reference the field of Critical Cartography, which emerged in the late 1980s as a reaction to what prominent geographers (in particular, J.B. Harley and Denis Wood) saw as a general complacency regarding the purported 'scientific objectivity' of maps:

"The theoretical critique of cartography addresses post-war academic cartography's search for ever better and more veridical representations of a pre-existing reality. But instead of participating in this search, critical cartography assumes that maps make reality as much as they represent it."[11]

In other words, maps not only reflect the power (state or other) of their creators to construct the reality they wish to see, but are themselves, as objects, powerful.[12] In Latin America, visual representation played a central role in the process of colonisation; by symbolically inventing the idea of 'New Spain', the land the Spanish 'discovered' became flat, ahistorical, ripe for possession.[13] This allowed them to impose their own order within an abstracted Cartesian grid which was decoupled from either landscape features or existing modes of life. The Spanish colonisers understood the power of maps to create a form of reality that they could control; after all, 'the products of power are not accuracy or truth but the acceptance and naturalisation of representations'.[14] In Lima, this colonial legacy can be clearly seen in the disconnect between landscape features, topography, and the form of the city; the colonial city has always turned its back towards its rivers and ignored its mountains.[15]

The idea that maps create reality has typically implicated the powerful and the elite as the creators of this reality: this includes not only colonisers but also contemporary state actors, militaries, and/or private-sector developers. As Harley put it, the 'ideological arrows have tended to fly largely in one direction.[16] Out of this context came the idea of 'counter-mapping', coined in 1995 by Nancy Peluso in a study examining forest mapping by indigenous communities in Indonesia. By appropriating the power of representation to create alternative realities, counter-mapping practices counterpose indigenous spatial ideas against those of the state[17] to make visible new understandings of territory. But the idea of counter-mapping – the way it was originally understood, at least – tends to assume that there is an existing, coherent understanding of the territory which is being given agency through the power of mapping, usually against the wishes of a more powerful

PUI Workshop participants discussing the border of their neighbourhood.

Source: Barrio Mio

7. For a description of this problem and Barrio Mio's approach to defragmentation, go to www.youtube.com/watch?v=okyk_pmtCLE

8. Franco, J.T. (2015). Espacios públicos amables para una ciudad informal, la experiencia de 'Barrio Mío en Lima, Archdaily.pe, Retrieved from http://www.archdaily.pe/pe/760924/espacios-publicos-amables-para-una-ciudad-informal-la-experiencia-de-barrio-mio-en-lima.

9. Brenner, N. (1999). Globalisation as reterritorialisation: The re-scaling of urban governance in the European Union. Urban Studies, 36(3), p. 432.

10. Kitchin, R., & Dodge, M. (2007). Rethinking maps. Progress in Human Geography, 31(3), 331-344.

11. Crampton, J.W & Krygier, J. (2005) An Introduction to Critical Cartography. ACME: An International E-Journal for Critical Geographies 4(1). p. 15.

12. Harley, J (1989) Deconstructing the Map, Cartographica. The International Journal for Geographic Information and Geovisualization 26(2). p. 12.

State. In Lima's periphery, this is not true: in fact, these neighbourhoods are characterised by extreme cultural diversity, a result of mass migrations from all corners of Peru over many decades. The work undertaken by Barrio Mio was then not to uncover and strengthen longstanding cultural understandings of territory but to create entirely new ones, to lead citizens in the creation of mappings that were simultaneously acts of politics and design. In that sense these projects exist in the gray zone between state-imposed planning and subversive counter-mapping.

Like the similarly-named and more well-known initiatives in Medellin, Colombia, the Barrio Mio program initiated Integral Urban Projects (PUI's), which in Lima correspond to 40 PUI 'zones' in the informal areas of Lima.[18] These zones, which are neighbourhood units large enough to have political impact and were determined in large part by natural topographical features and an extensive sociological study,[19] represent the re-scaling of much of Lima's periphery and, ideally, its political de-fragmentation. Before it was defunded, the Barrio Mio team of professional architects, planners, sociologists, economists and engineers succeeded in working with nine of these zones to begin developing cohesive urban visions that integrated circulation, public spaces, schools, libraries, health centres, housing and risk mitigation. The process involved multiple workshops with community members in which the goal was to facilitate, rather than lead.[20] Each PUI zone invariably included both flat areas and steep slopes.

To that end, Barrio Mio teams created images that distributed power democratically; rather than producing highly technical and 'pristine' cartographical representations of their newly defined neighborhoods, the images used and created during the workshops were accessible, simplified, even messy. The goal was to allow everyday citizens to feel like they had the power to contribute their own vision.[21] But because these workshops referenced territorial boundaries that had never existed, it was critical to create a form of representation that concretised this new reality - an easily referenced icon. These territorial diagrams acted like mental placeholders, a form of 'map as icon'[22] that constantly reinforced the newly created territorial boundaries. Simple, colourful graphics communicated to community members that they were now citizens of a new, larger unit. The 'map as icon' was necessary because the Barrio Mio workshops were attempting to accomplish two goals at once: to design, with the community, a vision for their neighbourhood, and in doing so to help them identify with their neighbourhood in the first place.

Making the Invisible Visible

At the metropolitan scale, the history of Lima is one of erasure: by violently imposing their own urban paradigms onto a landscape which was already territorialised, the Spanish actively destroyed existing modes of urban life, traces of which can be seen in the several hundred huacas, or pre-Hispanic holy sites, scattered like islands around

13. Craib, R.B. (n.d) Cartography and Power in the Conquest and Creation of New Spain. Latin American Research Review 35(1). p. 20.

14. Ibid., 22.

15. Ibid 2

16. Harley, B.J (2009) Maps, Knowledge, and Power: Geographic Thought-A Praxis Perspective. p. 300.

17. Rundstrom, R. (2009). "Counter-Mapping," International Encyclopedia of Human Geography (Amsterdam: Elsevier Science, 2009), 316.

18. Ibid 5. p. 27.

19. Ibid 16. p. 26.

20. Ibid 15

21. Ibid 20.

22. Stallmann, T, (2012). Alternative Cartographies Building Collective Power. University of North Carolina, Chapel Hill. p. 13.

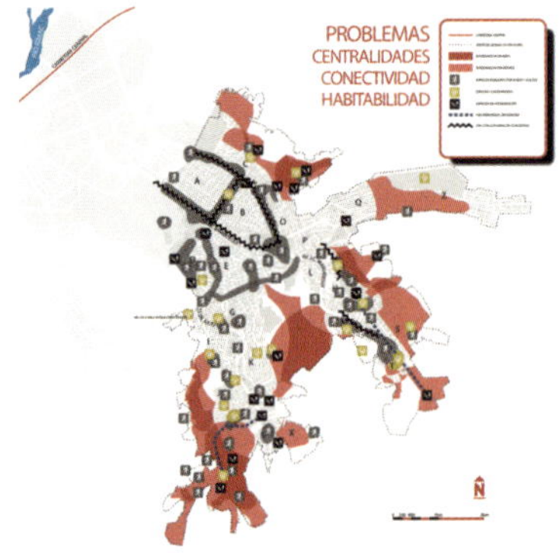

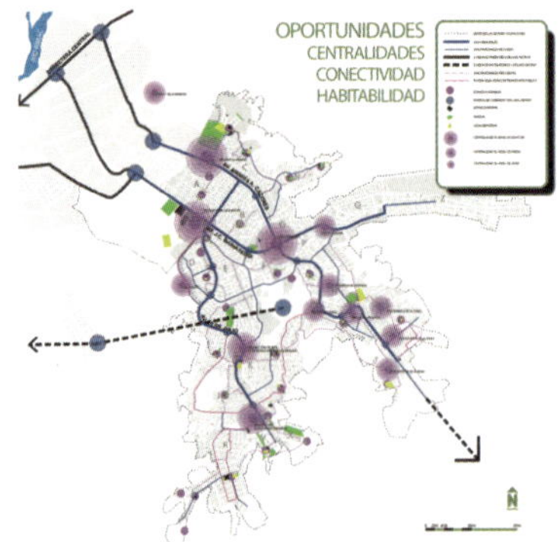

the city.[23] This predominant colonial mode of city building[24, 25] - suited for a flat topography - was never questioned, even as the state withdrew in the 1970s and waves of migrants began building on the steep slopes of the Andean foothills. In short, the lack of vision, of representations of alternative possible futures, produced a situation in which existing modes of colonial urbanism were simply continued even though they were increasingly inappropriate. The result has produced a catastrophic disconnect between the landscape and the city as well as a destructive complacency, in which it is assumed that the combination of steep slopes and position on the periphery must invariably be connected to extreme poverty (and that this is not the place for 'real' designers).

The Barrio Mio work has continued through a series of reports, studies, and a workshop in March 2016, the goal of which was to develop speculative visions for housing on the slopes of Lima.[26] These kinds of visions - somewhat utopian architectural and urban design projects that explicitly address topography - respond to this complacency with which citizens and designers alike view the periphery of Lima. Rather than accept the ingrained narrative, the images could be compared to what Geneviève Reid has referred to as *aspirational maps*, which draw connections between "...the landscape, the imagined landscape, and the digital landscape; between fixed maps and the dynamics of imagination".[27] In many cases the projects are inspired by pre-Hispanic Andean civilisations, many of which built cities on top of or buried into the sides of the mountains they revered as holy places.[28] The techniques they utilised (such as Inca terraces, which are often used to this day) represent practical alternatives to the problem of building on steep topographies. As Reid puts it, these kinds of alternative representations increase the 'capacity to aspire'; they provide suggestions and possibilities and encourage a broader conversation about urbanism that responds to landscape.

An implied goal behind the continued Barrio Mio work is to not only re-territorialise the city of Lima at the neighbourhood scale, but to re-centre (or, more accurately, to de-centre) it at the metropolitan scale. Similar to the ways in which diagrammatic representations of bounded territory concretise reality at the scale of the PUI zone, the speculative work at the metropolitan scale attempts to shift the dominant mental image of Lima from one of the colonial city surrounded by invisible slums to one in which the view is in fact from the mountaintop -

Above right:
Representations developed in Barrio Mio workshops to identify problems and opportunites.

Source: Barrio Mio Huaycan team

Above left:
Student project from Limapolis 2016 workshop (group 9, San Juan)

23. Huacas de Lima (City of Lima, n.d.). Retrieved from http://www.limacultura.pe/sites/default/files/publicaciones/mapa_huacas.pdf.

24. The Spanish 'Laws of the Indies' specified rules for colonial town planning, including the location of plazas, layout of streets, and locations of important elements like the church and the hospital.

25. Ibid 5. p. 7.

26. See the Limapolis 2016 conference/workshop website: http://facultad.pucp.edu.pe/arquitectura/eventos/limapolis-2016/

27. Reid, G., & Sieber, R. (2014) Aspirational Maps' and Indigenous Communities Conference Abstract Spatial Knowledge and Information CANADA. Retrieved from http://rose.geog.mcgill.ca/ski/system/files/fm/2014/reid.pdf.

Above:
Dangerous construction on steep slopes.

where living on the periphery becomes decoupled from assumptions of abject poverty.[29] If the periphery becomes 'centred' it becomes visible, folded into the territory of the city.

Contestations and Responsibilities

Despite the heroic tone of much of Barrio Mio - who, after all, can object to work that enables the poor to assert their rights? - the truth is that there is no clear dividing line between 'good' and 'bad' work, especially in such a messy, politically charged context. Within the discussions on counter-mapping, for instance, it is recognised that, due to complex relationships between 'oppressor' and 'oppressed', the results can be unpredictable and sometimes contradictory.[30] The situation in Lima is complicated by many factors, including the contradictions between the 'right to the city' and the fact that some families live in situations of un-mitigable risk. Who gets to determine new neighbourhood boundaries? Who gets to decide whether a family needs to be relocated? At the end of the day Barrio Mio was a government program and represented, for some, the unwelcome imposition of the state and the professional class.

Acknowledging the inherent contradictions and contestations within such work, however, only reinforces the importance of the image as a tool to develop politically active territories. The creators of the Barrio Mio program understood that, in Kevin Lynch's terms, the 'image of the city"[31] is not just the product of a lived experience or a design but also the shaper of that lived experience. To that end, mapmakers and urban designers who want to link Lima to itself have a vested interest in representing the city the way it actually exists, informal areas and all. Perhaps even more importantly, designers are those professionals who, through their ability to visually concretise abstract realities and create speculative visions, can shift conversations around what is even possible or desirable.

When the power inherent in images is recognised, it forces a degree of responsibility upon those who create and deploy them. The ways in which we represent our urban spaces to ourselves affect how we think about them and the people who live in them - and there are countless examples of this power being applied in the service of imperial, military or authoritarian goals. To that end, continued critical reflection about the latent power and political significance of the visual representation of territory is necessary, especially if the stated goal is to empower the invisible.

28. The Incas were not the only civilisation to find innovative ways to build on steep topographies; the Chachapoyas of northern Peru, for instance, built magnificent citadels on mountaintops and left the lowlands for farming. (See, for instance, the citadel of Kuelap).

29. Some speculative projects that arose out of the Limapolis 2016 workshop proposed a re-discovery of the Apu, or mountain spirit, in a process of re-sanctifying topographies that were historically the most sacred places in Peru.

30. Ibid 17. p. 316.

31. Lynch, K. (1960). The Image of the City. Cambridge, MA: MIT Press.

A CONVERSATION WITH Stuart Elden: Approaching Territory

What could be considered a standard definition of the concept of territory? And in what way could this be argued as limiting or inadequate when understanding particular environments both currently and in the future?

I think there have been, generally, two main ways that territory has been defined. The first is a fairly standard dictionary definition – a territory is a bounded space under the control of a group of people, perhaps a state or other political organisation. The second, which is not incompatible with the first, is that territory is the outcome of a process of territoriality – a human way of shaping and interacting with the environment. That second one can be based on animal ethology, and related to innate biological drive, or it can be a more socially based understanding of bounding, protecting, including and excluding. Much useful work can be and has been done with such definitions as starting points. But they, for me, get into problems when we try to unpack the definitions. The first might raise the questions that need to be asked – what is bounding, what is space, what kind of control, what kind of groups or political organisations? – but doesn't necessarily answer them. It also masks historical complexities – have we always worked in that way, in all human societies, and did people in the past understand the relation in the same way? The second also seems to lose sight of historical issues, and suggests that all human mechanisms towards the shaping, establishing and maintaining of territories can be understood through territoriality. It has also, for me, led to a lot of confusion where 'territory' and 'territoriality' are used almost interchangeably, and lead people to think that because there is literature on the second, we have an adequate theory of the first.

There is a great risk with territory, I think, of assuming that all societies have ordered things like us, with just the boundaries in different places and different regimes within them. Such issues would be increased if we tried to think about non-Western societies, so my question with different times and places would not be: how did they understand territory, or how did they practice it; but how did they understand and practice the relation between place, people and power?

The emphasis on boundaries in the standard definitions also presents problems when we look at contemporary issues. There was a lot of talk in the 1990s about boundaries disappearing, and that this perhaps meant that territory was becoming less significant. The notion of de-territorialisation, rather detached from its original context, was sometimes used to describe this. This could be in terms of Europe, or more broadly globalisation. Of course, with the migration currently taking place, and the building of walls across the world, such talk seems very outdated. But it was also conceptually misjudged. It failed to adequately address the ways that spaces were not being unregulated in the modern era, but being reshaped, and if the term de-territorialisation was to be used, it should also be balanced with an examination of re-territorialisation – looking at the breaking, rearrangement and remaking of socio-spatial relations, an on-going process rather than a static outcome.

Territory has also generally been understood in relation to static, dry land. But the land/sea relation complicates some of these ideas. Although many land territories use coastlines as their borders, states also claim significant parts of the sea or ocean. There is an established body of international law on this question. But as people like Phil Steinberg have pointed out, this becomes complicated when we look at ice, which can be solid or liquid at different times, blurring both geophysical states and legal regimes. Other geophysical issues also complicate this – coastal swamps or river deltas, glaciers, rivers, marshlands and so on. One of the key issues here is that these are dynamic features of the landscape, and so there are complications when we try to use them to demarcate political regimes, both practically and conceptually.

We assume this would be quite evident in the current case of the Arctic – could you perhaps elaborate these ideas with relation to your involvement in the ICE LAW project?

* The ICE LAW project ('Indeterminate and Changing Environments' / 'Law, the Anthropocene and the World') is a research project led by Philip Steinberg and the IBRU: Centre for Borders Research. This project is in its early stages with its initial focus being on the topic of ice and the legal issues surrounding it. 'Territory' is one of seven sub-projects, and is led by Stuart Elden.

Yes, and those kinds of issues are very much on my mind because of this project. And it is partly through this work, and initial conversations with Philip Steinberg and others that I've begun to think more seriously about the geophysical, the material. I've been brought into the project as much as a political theorist as a geographer, since there are already a number of geographers – both human and physical geographers – involved. At the project's initial conference, I began by saying that I was not surprised that people were finding traditional understandings of territory inadequate to understand issues around ice, the sea and so on. But as I've already said to you, part of the reason is that traditional understandings are also inadequate to grasp complexities around territory on land. So, rather than searching for a fixed definition, itself bounded, controlled and discrete, we would better to think about the different issues that were at stake in understanding territory in different environments, and let its sense and use emerge from that inquiry.

There are multiple things happening in the Arctic, which was the initial spur to this work. States are increasingly trying to map the sea bed, and using this as a basis of some of their territorial claims; the question of resources is sharpening the stakes; there are environmental issues and the impact of climate change. Because ice that was previously there year-round is now melting, either entirely or on a seasonal basis, new issues are emerging. Previously icebound areas are now open to shipping, and so for example to the north of Canada there are issues about what is internal waters, what open seas and what rights of navigation apply there. It has implications in terms of where people can live, migration routes for land and sea animals, availability of resources and so on. There have been some suggestions that we need an Arctic treaty like the one that applies to the Antarctic, which suspends territorial claims to that continent. But there are at least two crucial differences between the Antarctic and the Arctic. The Arctic has Indigenous populations who inhabit the land and ice that is being contested, whereas Antarctica's population is a transient one made up of scientists and environmentalists. And whereas Antarctica is a landmass with an ice sheet above and beyond it, the bulk of what is being contested in the Arctic is ice, open water or a mixture of the two, on a seasonal basis. There are of course landmasses within the Arctic, but the borders of those are largely fixed, even if there are remaining disputes. But as soon as you look at the water and ice, it becomes much more complicated, especially below the surface, into mineral resources and the seabed.

The notion of the border plays a particularly interesting role in this whole concept of territory. It insists some element of a spatial outcome. How significant is the border to a territory? Can territory exist without a border?

If we follow the traditional definition, then the border is crucial to territory, because the definition says that territory is a bordered or bounded space. But I'm not sure that it can be as simple as that. If putting a boundary around something creates a territory, then the term becomes so general as to be largely useless. So I've tried to get away from thinking that borders define territory.

One way to approach this is to think about what a border is. A border can be a simple line, marking the transition between one sovereign jurisdiction and another. This line has nominally zero width – you are either in one state or another. Most borders today take that form, sometimes called a boundary. But there are also borders which are much more gradual, more zonal, a region which you pass through between one state or political entity and another. This notion, often called a frontier, was more common historically. Today, generally, we think of the world-political map as these coloured units, with clear black boundary lines drawn around them, and that political power is often most effectively concentrated at those edges, for fortification and defence, control of movement of goods and people and so on. But historically, it makes more sense to think of political power as being concentrated in a key point, and spreading from that point to a greater or lesser extent, before fading out. There might be overlapping claims, or there might be a moment where it was clearly no longer the jurisdiction of one group and became that of another, but more common would be for there to be unclaimed areas.

A Greek polis, for example, would begin from the initial settlement, to controlling a larger area of land beyond the urbanised part, and then there might be a substantial gap before another human settlement. This understanding was common through the Middle Ages, with areas where there might be isolated human outposts, and then a lot of wilderness - marshes, forests, etc. - before the next civilised area. Now these might have boundaries of a sort - the walls of a city, the fences around cultivated land - but those lines wouldn't necessarily mark the limits of political authority. Even with the classical Roman Empire, they didn't see the walls or fortifications that they built as marking the final extent of expansion, but rather as a temporary stopping point. The famous Hadrian's Wall for example, was more to do with regulating movement and providing defence than it was a boundary marker - they moved further north and built another wall, land on both sides was cultivated. They certainly didn't see what was on the other side as having the same kind of political claim as they did.

For all these reasons it seems problematic to assume that territory can be defined by a boundary - and 'defined' is an interesting word in this case, because it comes from the Latin fines, which means a line or limit. To define is to put a boundary around something - it is this, and it isn't that. To think about territory in relation to my registers of enquiry - the economic, the strategic, the legal, the technical - doesn't mean that borders are unimportant. But I think it forces us to question how they are important, and what role they play. Property in land is interesting here, because there it becomes very important to mark out who claimed what and where. There are bodies of work by the Roman land surveyors which are important in seeing the techniques developed there - both legal, technical and economic. The Greek historian Herodotus tells the story of the original Egyptian geometers - the earth-measurers - who would be sent out each year after the Nile's floodwaters had subsided to mark out the boundaries of the fields anew. Work on fortifications and military techniques bridge the strategic and technical, and so on.

In the modern era, I've argued that the development of calculative technologies was important in understanding the development of territory, both as a concept and a practice. Political actors, and it increasingly became states, undertook large-scale land surveys, made accurate maps, developed population censuses, and so on. These made possible not only a much more detailed knowledge of what it was that they were claiming, but also the accurate marking out of borders. It's one thing to say that the border between two countries is a mountain range, and quite another to settle on which points form a boundary line. The 1659 Treaty of the Pyrenees, which brought an end to the fighting between France and Spain, is sometimes seen as beginning the process for the creation of the first modern boundary. Now, of course, boundary lines are marked with absolute precision, but it's important to remember that boundary-making is a process with stages. These are sometimes described as allocation, delimitation and demarcation, and my ex-colleagues at Durham's International Boundaries Research

Rather than searching for a fixed definition [of territory], itself bounded, controlled and discrete, we would be better to think about the different registers that were at stake, and let its sense and use emerge from that inquiry.

Unit used to say that a further stage of maintenance was important too. Today, the major work in boundaries concerns maritime boundaries, but there are still disputed boundaries on land.

So, while the territory-borders relation is crucial to understanding either, I don't think it is simple. A territory without borders is difficult to imagine, but I think it's a crucial first step to thinking about territory, breaking out of the simple dictionary-style definition. The way that territory is understood and practiced often leads to the kinds of borders that are created. A territory without boundaries is definitely possible, thinking of its borders as more zonal, transitional, or as what are often called frontiers. And in terms of the form that borders – as boundaries or frontiers – take, I think it's helpful to begin with asking questions about territory. Thinking about territory as a political counterpart of calculative space which makes possible the delimitation and demarcation of borders as boundaries, is, I think a valuable way forward. While territory might take on a strictly bordered form at particular times, looser, overlapping and multiple arrangements are also possible. So, rather than borders defining territory, territory helps us to understand borders. We can then understand the full range of political-spatial arrangements.

You discuss the relation between people, place and power with the scale of time. An additional scale could be that of the vertical, as we can consider a territory to be a make up of layers. What can be gained from a vertical analysis, or furthermore, a volumetric one?

Yes, I think this is crucial. In a piece in Political Geography in 2013 entitled 'Secure the Volume' I began to develop some ideas along these lines. As a starting point, the work by Eyal Weizman examines how Israel's occupation of the West Bank and Gaza needed to be understood through both military and civilian building projects, infrastructure and transportation networks. He argued forcefully that to understand the fractured and contested spaces of the West Bank we needed to think in three dimensions – not just the two dimensions of most cartographic imaginations. Surveying the work of others such as Stephen Graham and Bradley Garrett as well as some examination of particular sites I had visited in the West Bank and Israel, from the contested Area E1 to Israel's border with Lebanon at Rosh Hanikra, emphasised the importance of this vertical dimension. I tried to link the vertical – work on airspace, height and things above the surface – with work examining what was going on underground.

Additionally, what I tried to do in the piece was to break from just thinking of a simple up-down axis added to the two dimensional way of thinking. It was for this reason that the idea of volume appealed, trying to break from ideas of planes, areas or surfaces. I borrowed the notion of the 'volumetric' from cartography – because the volumetric seemed to work in two ways: to bring in the notion of volume, and three-dimensions, but also the metric, as a means of understanding a calculative space. There are also some interesting discussions about slopes, the oblique, texture and the materiality of space in three dimensions that I thought added to discussions simply of the vertical.

Kerb:
How then, have you tried to approach territory?

What I have tried to do in my two books on territory – Terror and Territory and The Birth of Territory – is to abandon the quest for a single, ahistorical definition of territory, and instead to ask: how can we understand how place-people-power relations were labelled, conceptualised and practiced in different times and places? Some of these would be close to how we now understand territory, but not necessary all. To do so I suggested that we interrogate these relations in a range of registers. Politics and geography are obviously crucial, but I suggested that we look at economic, strategic, legal and technical issues. I'd broaden this today to put more emphasis on the geophysical and the geocorporeal – the bodies in these spaces – as well. There may be other registers people would want to add, the social-cultural, for example. But even if the ones I have emphasised are seen as too limited, I think this approach helps us to understand some of the complexities of territory.

SURFACE TENSION

TERRI WARPINSKI

Standing in a solitary stretch of desert full of ocotillo, rock and dirt on a freshly scraped road, a brand new steel fence rose up out of the ground more than three times my own (substantial) height and extended in both directions as far as my eyes could see - a distance of more than 25 miles. Just fence and road and open desert.

It was 2009. The new US border fence had just been put into place along 580 miles of the Mexican border at a cost reported to be 1-4 million US dollars per mile. And, at the very same time, the world was celebrating the twentieth anniversary of the fall of the Berlin Wall! How could this be?

These questions would launch a five year photographic project spanning three continents to bring together three regions where the landscape was radically altered by the construction of physical barriers to demarcate and enforce geo-political borders. On that occasion I was not only thinking about the border fence before me, but also remembering Israel's plan to physically protect its citizens with a separation barrier to effectively seal off the Palestinian Territories.

A few months after that moment of reckoning along the border fence in Arizona I visited Berlin, and from there made the first of several return visits to Israel and the Palestinian Territories. In Berlin I was eager to understand the many ways in which the Berlin Wall - through its formal monuments, casual remnants, and in some instances, its complete erasure - affected the fabric of the landscape. What I found in Berlin was a mending urban landscape still dominated by the wall, which, in its absence and among its fragmented remains, continues to be a powerful presence in the city. Its imprint keeps its memory alive, and encourages the citizens of Berlin, of Germany and of the world to maintain awareness of how we resolve political and cultural tensions. I was fascinated by architect Rem Koolhaas' description of the Berlin Wall 'as a masterpiece whose symbolic effects were infinitely more powerful than its physical appearance', and speculated whether or not similar effects occur within the context of our twenty-first century border constructions.

The photographs in Surface Tension: Three Landscapes of Division contrast and parallel the contemporary border constructions between the United States and Mexico with the division between Israel and the Palestinian Territories. Berlin serves as a both a prologue/ precedent and epilogue/postscript

Perhaps the most significant aspect of creating and maintaining a social/ political border is the power to define what lies on the other side; to have the power to determine what belongs versus what is alien. In borderlands, if we look for it, we can find relationships between center and periphery, security and insecurity, state and society, territory and belonging, politics and identity. In language, boundaries or borders assume fixity, when in actuality they are spaces of dynamic movement and great complexity where two (or more) realities can be experienced/witnessed/ observed simultaneously. Bordering, as a process, can be illustrated by an example from the settlement of the American West. In 1890 the American Census Bureau declared that it could no longer chart the westward movement of the US Frontier because the western boundary had 'dissolved'. There were simply too many pockets of settlements that were now scattered across the west that they effectively broke up and blurred any clear line of demarcation. A similar phenomenon is at work in the Palestinian Territories with the disappearance of land that has occurred through the repeated breaching of the Green Line (the 1949 Armistice Agreement boundary between Israel and the Palestinian Territories) by illegal settlements of Israeli citizens. These repeated violations clearly show where the balance of power resides and have all but erased anything resembling a clear demarcation of the border.

Israel /Palestine
Under Settlement [Hebron]

Here, over the old Palestinian marketplace in the center of Hebron, the Israeli settlers of Avraham Avinu live in the upper stories of the buildings that line the streets. The scene I depict occurs deep in the souk (market), where at one point, the tarp that shades the heat of the sun from pedestrians below is missing. Revealed overhead a wire mesh 'fence' put in place by the Palestinians to hold back massive amounts of detritus – including rocks and cement blocks, garbage, furniture, metal objects, even bags of feces – that have all been launched out of the windows, doors, and from the rooftops of the Israeli settlement down on to the Palestinian pedestrians below.

Israel/Palestine
Above left:
Checkpoint 300 [Bethlehem]

Above middle:
Walled In [Abu Dis]

Above right:
Descent [East Jerusalem]

Berlin
Far left top:
Interventions [Typology]

Far left bottom:
Whitewashed

Following images:
Into the Wild [Along the Mauerweg]

My creative practice has always focused on the relationship between personal, cultural and natural histories as revealed through the landscape. The landscape as a site is the intersection of nature and culture, and as such bears the inscription of the human narrative on its surface. I see the landscape, then as a palimpsest, with its multiple layers showing evidence of change over time.

My most recent projects have been driven by the conviction that, in many instances, a border is as much a process as it is a physical location – as a structure, a border begins as an idea, an abstraction that can be simplified to a line on a map. This line is a conscious human determination. It is a decision. Its consequences are many, be they social, political, environmental, economic or psychological, extending down to the individual person as well as incurring global effects and, as with any decision, over time, radical change is possible.

US /Mexico
As Far as the Eye Can See
[East of Naco]

A CONVERSATION WITH Geography & Memory:

Joanne Garde-Hansen & Owain Jones

You reference memory as "not simply the burden of the past" but as key to the process of becoming. In this way memory becomes operative. Can you elaborate on this?

We spent some time considering the structure of the collection Geography and Memory (2012) as the set of a stage that we wanted our contributors to negotiate, and agreed these as scales of identity, place and becoming. We were keen to shift the focus in memory studies from a temporal framework focused on trauma and history, which has defined much of European explorations of cultural memory as 'burden', to one in which everyday place, space, landscape and environment has a bearing on individual remembering, forgetting and becoming. One aspect of our way of approaching memory sees memory as continually materialised and resourced in a whole range of constructive ways. As such, to remember and to forget is to perform an operation on the past in the present moment, but it is also to administer the past, and perform the present, even if only through some sort of personal policy of sorting out our memories. To see it in operational terms then is to acknowledge that in the all-important business of performing personal, cultural and collective identities, there are underlying economies of remembering and forgetting that need to be addressed through what one might call a politics of administration of memory, rather than simply a politics of recognition of one's identity through one's right to memory (to borrow these concepts from political science).

How important is narrative in describing identity and connection to place? Does the act of attributing narrative solidify identity?

Memory work does entail a continuous weave of simultaneously realised stories of oneself in relation to place: where one is from, where one is right now, where one is going; in relation to others around you (and maybe, not around you). This is a dynamic, connective and mobile process - some might even argue transitory process, particularly for younger people who may feel less fixed to place and more connected to multiple places and identities. It seems to be the case that if one cannot create a convincing story - or set of stories - about oneself in the contexts of everyday life - economy and culture - then 'solid' or at least robust identities are at risk. When the coal mining industry in the UK was very rapidly (in historic terms) wound down there were, sadly, many suicides amongst younger men who were made redundant. Their narrative of self in the context of memories of powerful community and family identities were challenged to the point of breakdown. Yet, this is a narrative of trauma, and one often told, that is countered by narratives of resilience, class-war, and entrepreneurialism as in the example of the film Dark Horse (2015), about a post-industrial Welsh mining village, who build a new collective memory around their syndicate that breeds a prize-winning racehorse from one of the most deprived parts of the United Kingdom.

The relationship between the body and topography affects a kind of transference. How does this transference shape identity?

The transference works both ways, from the human to nonhuman and back and forth. Affect is fundamentally about interactions. Our becoming human identity is received (a sort of act of recognition) by our environment (even if we do not always recognise our environment), and we remember and (sometimes strategically) forget the environment. The topographies, and the marks we have made in the landscape either directly or indirectly, are remembered. We know as we walk the fields or the streets that the landscape is shaped by our consumption, it remembers us and our footsteps at the time and our future needs - food, water, energy, big data. This is a personal recognition as well as a collective responsibility to the relationship we (all) have with our bodies, the relationship our bodies have to topography, and this may be more transactional than transference, a new metabolism of body and topography. There will always be some sort of exchange. As Iain Sinclair wrote about the poet John Clare who lost his land and then his self, and the transformations to 'his' East London for the 2012 Olympic Park, if known/loved topographies are changed violently and radically then the self can be challenged. "This is what I feel about this landscape. I've walked out into it so often that it accepts me. Bits of stone and river accept me, and I know myself by that. If the landscape changes, then I don't know who I am either. The landscape is a refracted autobiography. As it disappears you lose your sense of self". This must be most acutely felt by communities who have no time to adapt to the changes in their environment wrought by natural disasters.

How important is scale when exploring the topic of geography and memory? What can we discover about the impacts on identity from an individual perspective? Does the exploration of small scale relationships inform the larger collective scale?

Scale is very important, perhaps now more than ever. Memory studies have been largely framed by national questions, frames, contexts and this scale is productive but also reductive in a globally mediated landscape. Keightley and Pickering have recently discussed inter-scalarity of memory, and in our own work we have researched micro, meso, and macro scales of memory (in relation to water) in order to explore where the gaps in research are. The personal and human scale still lacks enough attention in geography and memory studies. So rather than the individual which assumes separation from the collective, much of our thinking on memory approaches the personal-communicative aspects of remembering as a form of mapping the self in relation to bigger scales and processes: a multi-scalarity of memory. This may be less about the small scale informing the large scale and more about the personal human story of the self in itself as a form of intangible heritage. And this scale has leverage. A big question remains about the role of the lived, performed body and all its affective, sensing moving procedures in relation to memory creation and expression, and the networked digital worlds of culture and economy that operate to create and express.

You describe the connection between memory and who we are as being wrapped up in memories of our past present and future and these connections being hard to pin down and slippery. How important is placement in time when describing these relationships?

Because memory is such an essential, ubiquitous, every-moment function, it is easy to pass over just how complex and mysterious it is as a process – or set of processes. We do not run memory. It runs us, and it is always doing so in relation to the body and the place the body is in. Thus, placement is key. It seems to be the case that everyday becoming is, to a large degree, a matter of routine in which memory is quietly at work in a complex relation to the senses and immediate consciousness. It is only when novelty crops up – say in the home – or place of work – or self-imposed, where attention, perception and consciousness take control back from the 'automatic pilot' of routine memory. But the relationships between placement, time and practice is, again, much more uncertain and complex than immediately apparent. Memories in the form of reveries (daydreams) and Déjà vu (sudden vivid flash-backs) show what could be described as convection currents in deep memory, where our relationships to self, place and time are always gently – or violently – weaving and reweaving deep within our becomings.

In discussing territory, identity is commonly discussed in terms of national identity. Is there a danger in describing identity in general terms? Does this have the potential to dismiss a finer complexity?

As a number of people have argued, there is an active hostility to 'place' in Western philosophy, politics and culture. The destruction of place and the forcing of people from place is a necessary means for the production of modernity. National identity does have a privileged place in modern politics as it is used to secure the State. Often collective memory is retro-engineered and negatively inflected to do this. The 'universal human rights' bestowed on us by the United Nations convention is a 'right to nationhood' not a right to place, or community, or family, or region, or bio-region. UNESCO offers a 'right to heritage' but not a 'right to memory'. Most people's identities are not primarily formed through knowledges, practices and memories of 'the State' though in some extreme circumstances that may be the case. Those seeking a move to meaningful forms of ecological sustainability often call for a re-focusing of identity, politics and economy on 'place' in which deep memory plays a part and which offers new forms of administration (i.e. custodianship, collaboration, preservation, conservation etc). This might pay other dividends too in our urgent need to actualise non-modernity.

Images:
Courtesy of Andrew Holmes
2015

A CONVERSATION WITH Rene Peralta: On The Border

There are no scripts to follow at the border region. My work has involved many collaborations and mediums that engage the complexity of this place. Film, texts, and urbanism have been the instruments to catalogue and document the dynamic urban development at both sides of the border.

What role do you see national borders playing in a world where borders are traversed through international flows such as global trade, vast communications networks and international corporate ownership?

To some people the notion of state or nation seems to be an abstract idea, meaning they know they are in, or belong in one, because they have a document or pay taxes, etc. As the author Benedict Anderson states, a nation 'is an imagined political community'. Where I come from, the US/Mexico Border, the Tijuana/San Diego region, you can grasp the physical extent of nation through experiencing its limits via a border fence, which highlights the difference in urban praxis and the inconsistencies of working in a shared geography. I have also had the opportunity to see urban outcomes that characterise the Information Age, which are dramatically present in this border region of Tijuana/San Diego (one of North America's fastest-growing and more dynamic borderlands). Tijuana is globally engaged through the presences of the maquiladora (assembly-plant) industry, a hemispheric trade in trafficking, and its locus as the busiest international boundary crossing in the world (six million crossings a year). Now the role of the border region between San Diego/Tijuana is about paradoxical effects. Those same effects are what produce interactions and evade the idea of the postmodern idea of integration. Yet there are breaches to the border through the networks of flows of capital, trade and even human and drug trafficking. Again, the border is a space of paradoxical encounters, far from achieving synthesis or disappearing.

What potentials and difficulties does the 'edge' condition of the border between the US and Mexico provide for architects, and at what scales do these arise?

As we move back and forth across 'La Linea' (the line as the border is imagined) the relationships and strategies between geography and urban development is dealt with quite differently due to structural differences between both regions and countries. Challenges for architects and urbanists within this region include rethinking the shared geography as a step toward new urban policies that could blur strict boundaries. Since the demarcation of the US/Mexico border, the actual limit and physical edge between these two countries has gone through several processes of speculation, bartering and 'transaction' that have defined the planning and cultural mythologies of its urban regions. Within these interchanges and contradictions, the geography of the region has been a participant in the incessant dialogues of political and territorial debate. For example, water in most parts of the US/Mexico border region is a shared preoccupation since the Colorado River supplies a significant amount of cubic meters to the urban regions of Mexicali/Calexico and Tijuana/ San Diego. Tributaries that bifurcate from the river extend and cross national borders throughout their trajectory. Similar to the exchange of goods and labor, the issue of water rights and treatment has been subjected to bi-national politics that affect the future development and growth of these cities. As urban and industrial development increases in the name of modernisation (through relaxed environmental laws and policies), ecological systems are at the brink of collapse. The subjugation of formal and informal development of the south, which in the last 20 years has reached its critical mass, demands an urgent revisit to the geography and sustainability of the region.

What differences or similarities do you see in this border situation compared to others around the world?

I have noticed more difference than similarities. The San Diego/Tijuana border is a contested territory like many other border regions, yet the disparities somehow seem to build integral relationships rather than separate them. To other academics the border wall is described as a mode of aggression and therefore might bring similarities with the Palestine/Israel border. But it's not the case, there are ways in which the differences get resolved and the balance of diversity can still be maintained.

Your recent research has been directed towards social and cultural forms of the border city, how do you see these forces contributing to a re-making of territory in Tijuana and San Diego?

I have been interested in how concepts of cultural hybridity (Canclini) resonate with local writers and artists, who began creating work that represented the struggles within the forces that defined the city at the end of the twentieth century. For instance, works by installation artist Marcos Ramirez, 'ERRE', showcased the political conflicts between two countries and two cultures that were seeking (at least practically) to become interconnected. At the bi-national art event INSITE 94, Ramirez constructed a small self-built home similar to those found in squatter developments; it was installed in the main plaza of the Tijuana Cultural Center, a component of the Rio Zone urban redevelopment plan of the 1970s and distinguished by a strong modernist and monumental formal architecture. The two structures in juxtaposition represented the discordant realities brought about by modern industry and nationalism, and the constricting effect it had in defining Tijuana's hybridity. An alternative view of a postmodern idea of hybridity came from a young writer/philosopher, Heriberto Yepez, who argued that Tijuana does not define itself through fusion or synthesis, but instead through its contrasts and contradictions. In Made in Tijuana, Yepez writes:

"It's the asymmetry, stupid. The asymmetry, get it? The Fusion does not define Tijuana, but its contrast. Process City //of post-synthetic dialectics// antinomian laboratory of the glocalisation. Maquilandia+Farmaceuticals+Migration = Polemic Metaphors".

Confronting these debates, sometimes in their interstices, a new generation of Tijuana writers, artists and musicians have integrated their work into what is known as 'Art from the North,' a definition that moved from Fronterizo to just being Norteño. The imposed consciousness that was inherent in the government-inspired Mexicanisation projects of the 1970s as well as the rhetoric of globalisation – promising a kind of Hegelian national synthesis – failed because it was a fundamental misconception of the border by national as well as international investors and media. Tijuana remains true to nothing more than itself.

In the last five years Tijuana has made resilient efforts to move away from a drug cartel hegemony that plagued it. This terrorism, the recombination of culture and excess of freedom, had created an environment or an urbanism of illegality in spatial terms. This architecture of ambiguity or DIY Urbanism is now, I believe, being replaced with the desire of a more familiar market driven development – unfortunately the hybrid cultural praxis has surrendered to the city, embracing the global neoliberal trap of progress and security.

You propose a solar and algae farm for the Tijuana river as a way of revitalising the region. Do you see energy, and in particular renewable energy, influencing territories in the future?

The Tijuana River Canal was built to relieve flooding in the surrounding urban areas of the city by channeling rain and surface water to the Pacific Ocean. The canal is an outdated mono-functional infrastructure based on 40 year-old urban technology. Currently, deportees from the U.S use it as temporary shelter, living in unsafe and unsanitary conditions.

With highways on both sides of the canal, private and commercial vehicle traffic increase CO2 levels on adjacent residential and commercial areas. Furthermore, the water discharged into the canal only receives secondary treatment and it's sent to the ocean, affecting the Tijuana River Estuary and coastal waters of both Tijuana and San Diego beaches.

By the integration of solar energy farms via PV Panels spanning the width of the canal it is possible to regenerate the Tijuana River Canal into large-scale energy producing infrastructure.

The social benefits of the Tijuana Solar River include its capacity to generate renewable energy for a large sector of the population, the reduction of greenhouse gases and the ability to reclaim water in a drought-ridden region. The Tijuana Solar River Project also offers the possibility for a 40 year-old canal to become an asset to the city and promote Tijuana as a twenty-first century sustainable city.

The original canal was a symbol of the intent to bring control from the state (Mexico City) to the periphery (Tijuana); now this project is an opportunity to use the canal as an instrument for autonomy for the city of Tijuana and the region. Culturally, we have experienced a break from national hegemony and the border has forged its own identity.

The Solar River project tries to establish a new kind of urban sovereignty based on the technologies of the twenty-first century.

What does the border produce?

The novelist Raymond Chandler once wrote that Tijuana is not Mexico.

And the towns and later cities of Mexico's northern border began at a distance in spatial and historical terms. Places like the San Diego/Tijuana border are a mere 170 years old while other cities in the country can brag of longevity of more than 700 years. Because of this late development the border area produced a collaged identity between US and Mexican tropes. From the Chicano of the US side to the Fronterizo on the Mexican side.

The border created its own utopias – utopias away from national sentiment – and in other cases it allowed the creation of a fictional world. The border produced its own rules in defining Mexican or US culture. Literature, music, visual arts and other cultural praxis were all re-territorialised, constructing a post-Mexican sentiment. Today this is a vision of a border that navigates outside modernity in a plethora of images depicting the heterogeneous make up of its cities, all a product of the coming of age in the middle of postmodern conditions.

OBSERVATION

S E R

O S RV IO

SE V TI N O ERV ION O ERV ION

OBSERVATION

S O E

OBSE ATI N

OBSERVATION

O S RV IO

OBSE ATI N

SE V TI N O ERV ION O ERV ION

OBSERVATION

S E

SE V TI N O ERV ION O ERV ION

OBS RVAT ON

S E

SE V TI N O ERV ION O ERV ION

SE V TI N O ERV ION O ERV ION

S E

OBSERVATION OBSERVATION OBSERVATION

ATION OBSERVATION

T I

BS VA I N

OBS E VA I N OBS E VA I N O SE V ATI N

OBSERVATION

TION

T I

OBSERVATION

ERVATION ERVATION OBSERVATION

OBSERVATION

OB ER VA I N OB ER VA I N O SE V TI N

BS VA I N

OBSERVATION

O EP TIO

OBS E VA I N OBS E VA I N O SE V ATI N

OBSERVATION

TION

T I

ATION

ATION

OBS E VA I N OBS E VA I N O SE V ATI N

ATION OBSERVATION

T I O

BS VA I N

OBS E VA I N OBS E VA I N O SE V ATI N

O ER TIO

OBSERVATION

OBS E VA I N OBS E VA I N O SE V ATI N

T I

OBSERVATION OBSERVATION OBSERVATION

O TIO

David Heymann

DEFINING THE TERRITORIES OF LANDSCAPE PRACTICE: TOWARDS THE NEO-INFRASTRUCTURAL

The Sublime Landscape:
The Birth of the Faux- Paradisiacal
Landscape
(Image by the author, May 2016, after
Botticelli, The Birth of Venus, 1486)

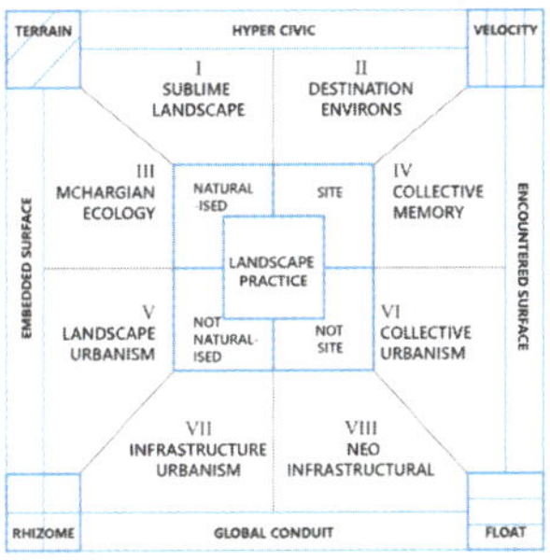

Territories Within the Expanded Field of Landscape Practice.
(Image by the author, May 2016).

Prologue

In this epoch of rapid change, unknown futures and the Anthropocene, the way in which we understand and design for the various territories of landscape must critically shift. In the hype of post-modernity, we have lost site (and sight) of the true rendering of landscape.
We hero the sanitisation of parks, the museumification of history and the romanticisation of nature.

A landscape territorium mortuus.

Dead territory...

Fifty years after McHarg and Companies 'Declaration of Concern',[1] Richard Weller asks:

Has landscape Architecture failed?[2]

Arguably, yes. However, only insofar as it has been working within the wrong territories. This article is a visual and written journey through these suggested territories of landscape practice.[3]
It presents an exploration, critique and proposed future for practice in two parts:

Part One: Stuck in a Territorium Mortuus (I–VI)

Part Two: Toward the Neo-Infrastructural (V–VIII)

A note on territory and the Expanded Field: territory (within a practice) is invention + accident.[4]

Put simply invention is the designer(s) (or not designers) of the site (or not site), the narrative and discussion. This cannot be fixed and undoubtedly crosses other territories. The accident is the corresponding output, users, conversation, media coverage, debate, programming and change over time (immanent destruction). This may be embedded in site, but is inherently in flux with time and space. Accidents can be grouped, and thereafter expressed (or positioned) within a greater theoretical framework (the Expanded Field). The Expanded Field of Landscape Practice[5] presents a theoretical assemblage by which to test, challenge and discover new territories within a practice.

By way of journeying through the Expanded Field, this article concludes that we must shift from the hyper civic territories manifesting in the north to one embodying the epistemologies of the twenty-first century in the south. Beyond aesthetic commodity, toward the Neo-Infrastructural.[6]

Part One: Stuck in a Territorium Mortuus

Territory I: Sublime Landscapes

'...landscape architecture is a profession limited to the production of small, rarefied sites such as gardens, parks, and plazas...landscape architecture is... a public art.'

Richard Weller[7]

Welcome to paradise!

The Sublime Landscape emanates the conditioning of place through the true rendering of 'high' (hyper civic) aesthetics. Materialising from the ideals of the 'garden as paradise' (after the Moghuls, the Persians, etc.), it delivers overtly indulgent, experiential, and idyllic landscapes. It is the fantastical and manicured work of landscape Starchitects, those who pertain to a 'representational imperative' reflective of the 'heroic ego of the individual.'[8] Calling upon Kantian aesthetics,[9] they are undeniably beautiful, albeit inherently static. A painted landscape. A faux paradisiacal impossibility. A Peter Walker + Martha Schwartz meets Le Notre's Versailles concoction. Whilst we cannot (and should not) deny the enjoyment and 'beauty' of these picturesque landscapes, we must look beyond this façade of divinity, to the less dignified realities beyond. We should not champion landscapes (and define the profession) by a territory principled in momentary indulgences. A fallen apple... not a fruitful orchard.

Territory II: Destination Environs

'Junkspace is picturesque, is Disney... it cannot be grasped, it cannot be remembered...the picturesque is now wrested from the homogenised, the singular liberated from the standardised...more and more is more.'

Rem Koolhaas[10]

Luxury lifestyle narratives ahead!

Landscape architecture has become a commodity toolkit. A set of standardised, repeated semiotics. A theme park for assumed sustainability and green-wash realities. Gentrified High Lines of

1. McHarg, I et. al. (1966). A Declaration of Concern, Landscape Architecture Foundation. Retrieved from http://lafoundation.org/about/delcaration-of-concern/.

2. See: Weller, R & Fleming, B. (2016). Has Landscape Architecture Failed? Reflections on the occasion of the 50th Anniversary of The Landscape Architecture Foundation, The Dirt, p.5. Retrieved from https://dirt.asla.org/2016/03/23/has-landscape-architecture-failed/.

3. The written component presents an overview of the given territories by way of critique and discussion. The visual component plays on the notion of the 'painted landscape' (a common practice in landscape architecture) by overlaying aspects of the territory on top of famous renaissance landscapes. The very essence of 'revival' or 'rebirth'.

4. For every invention (e.g. Ship) there must also be a subsequent accident (Shipwreck) stems from the philosophy inherent with speed, technology and space from Virillio. See Virilio, P (2007). The Original Accident, Polity Press, Cambridge, p.10.

5. The expanded field is a highly theoretical assemblage that cannot be explained in full here. However, its framing follows the rationale presented initially by: Kraus, R. (1979). Sculpture in the Expanded Field, October, Vol. 8 Spring, pp. 30-44 ; and thereafter in Infranet Lab & Lateral Office (2011). Pamphlet Architecture 30: Coupling, Princeton Architectural Press, New York, p. 8.

6. The Neo -Infrastructural, is a territory developed initially in the author's masters thesis see: Heymann, D (2014). Beyond Petroleum, Visions of a Future Hulkscape, Masters of Landscape Architecture Thesis, The University of Melbourne; available online at: www.pigeondesigndelivery.com

Destination Environ:
Return of Consumers to the Imperial 'Green' Façade.
(Image by the author, May 2016, after Canaletto, Return of Bucentoro to the Molo, 1729)

picturesque amnesia; a '[green] mask upon the imperial façade.'[11] Destination Environments[12] display a representational imperative that forgo the social lessons of Marcel Lefebvre, Jane Jacobs, David Harvey and others.[13] Intentionally or not, the territory puts capitalist (post-Fordist) programming before a public social reality. Throughout the Hyper Civic (global north), landscape projects have fallen endemic to this homogenising territorial aesthetic. It has become the normative output. The shiny-make-feel-nice generic rhetoric being regurgitated out of universities and practices alike.

Void of context, they are designs for the lucky few, the 'bourgeois', and the inherently bland. This is bad design. It is socially unethical. It is junk-space. Failing to critically consider the future resilience required for a growing (or shrinking) city, by championing a one size fits all, representational-imperative.

Territory III: McHargian Ecology

'...[ecological advocacy] is nothing more than a rear guard defence of a supposedly autonomous 'nature' conceived to exist a priori outside of the human agency or cultural construction.'

Charles Waldheim[14]

Easy to install, ready-made ecology!
Buy one swale, get a wetland free!

From the proprietors of the Bush School dreamers, to the Walling naturalists, the impetus to recreate nature (and subsequent denial of 'God's Junkyard'[15]), has proven an ineffective, but commonly practiced Territory. We cannot (and never could) recreate nature through design. Yet remarkably, we still appear to be trying. Take Peter Walkers recent proliferation: Barangaroo.[16] This continual desire for landscape to prove itself as the territorial proprietor of 'the natural', has become a tiring rhetoric. Nature is (by its very nature!) far more resilient than humans will ever be.[17] It just might not pertain to the type of 'nature' we uphold... No matter how many times we dust off the institutionalised Design With Nature.[18] Landscape practice is not, and will never be, the 'saviour' of the worlds devastated environments. Weeds will grow and cockroaches will roam. We need to shift our focus to dealing with the inconceivable mess we've made of this planet, rather than continually trying to recreate an ecology rendered obsolete.

Territory IV: Collective Memory

'History corrupts; absolute history corrupts absolutely. Bland has become the only meeting ground for the old... the formerly residual is declared the essence, the focus of intervention.'

Rem Koolhaas[19]

Who wants to be swept away in an awe of landscaped nostalgia?

Somewhere between the indefinite heterotopias of time,[20] and the obsessive inventory of forms, the museumification

7. Weller referring to the sentiments of Peter Walker as a 'landscape artist.' Ibid. 2, p. 5.

8. Allen, S. (1999). Infrastructure Urbanism. Points + Lines: Diagrams and Projects for the City. Princeton Architectural Press, New York, p. 52.

9. See Immanuel Kant's 1790 philosophy on the aesthetics of beauty in Critique of Judgement

10. Koolhaas, R. (2004). Junk-space. Content. Taschen, New York, p.170

11. As Mumford puts it in; Mumford, L. (1924; 1955). Sticks and Stones: A Study of American Architecture & Civilization, Boni & Liveright. New York, p. 438.

12. The term 'Destination Environment' coined in; Waldheim et.al. (2008). Logistics Landscapes. Landscape Journal, Vol. 27, iss. 2, p. 220.

13.In reference to classic Marxist/social theory considering the right to the city. See by way of example David Harvey's classic: Harvey, D. (1989) The Condition of Post Modernity.

14. Waldheim, C. (2006). Landscape Urbanism. Landscape Urbanism Reader. Princeton Architectural Press, New York, p. 38

15. As McHarg tactfully puts it in regard to the state of the city as noted in Blake, P. (1964) God's Own Junkyard: The Planned Deterioration of America's Landscape, Rinehart & Winston, New York.

16. The discussion and critique around Barangaroo is an essay in its own right. As a starting point, see the recent issue of Landscape Architecture Australia, iss 149. And for a good introductory critique see: Wallis, J. (2012) The Politics of Aesthetics: Expanding the critique of Headland Park Sydney, JOLA, Autumn, pp. 64-71.

17. See, by way of example, natures inherent resilience at Chernobyl; Wendle, J. (2016) Animals Rule Chernobyl 30 Years After Nuclear Disaster, National Geographic Online. Retrieved from http://news.nationalgeographic.com/2016/04/060418-chernobyl- wildlife-thirty-year-anniversary-science/

18. See of course, McHarg, I. (1969, 1992). Design With Nature 25th Anniversary Edition, John Wiley & Sons, New York.

Landscape Urbanism:
Sprawling Landscape
(Image by the author, May 2016, after Goyen, Dune Landscape, 1630)

of site/sight has stayed a legitimate territory within landscape. The 'folly' is by no means a new idea. From Roman ruins to faux-Chinoiserie pagodas in English landscapes, the romanticisation of dilapidated objects (contextually removed) has been a common practice.

Today however, they reflect the designed rediscovery of a static moment, captured and museumified. The botanic garden (museum for plants); cemetery (museum for the dead); memorial (museum for events); the post-industrial (museum for expelled industries). The latter and most problematic of these is the post-industrial. A post-modern delusion that glamorises previously industrial sites,[21] ignorantly denying productive realities. Whilst we foray in the so-called 'ruins' of soot-covered yesteryear we ought not to forget the (out of site/sight) mega-refineries, factories and plants consuming vast expanses of landscape to meet our consumption demands. Memory is important. However, the way in which it is presented should not be through a lens of semiotics and nostalgia, singular in invention, romantic in accident.

***

Part Two: Towards the Neo Infrastructural

Territory V: Landscape Urbanism

'[We must] shift a good amount of attention away from small scale site design in order to consider how we can improve regional landscape deficiencies of the urban realm.'

Alan Berger[22]

For the leaders of Landscape Urbanism,[23] the 'failings' of landscape stemmed from its inability to see the bigger picture. This was however, a reoccurring occupation for the modernist planners: Howard's Garden City; Corbusier's Radiant City; Wright's Broad Acre, etc.

Landscape Urbanism stepped back from the overarching utopianism of the city plan, and reverted to the green-field 'stim' and subsequent 'drosscape'[24] of urbanity and sprawl. Through evocative mapping and landform based analysis, this territory creates arguably idealistic master plans of 'McHargian' wetlands and swales, covering vast regions. Landscape urbanism is as outdated as the redundant use of the master

Collective Memory:
Museumification within the
Ruins of Nostalgia.
(Image by the author, May 2016, after Lorrain, Capriccio with Ruins of the Roman Forum, 1634)

plan. While sprawl is a critical issue, promoting a one-stop solution through this landscape territory is not the answer. We need to work with other disciplines (like planning and architecture...yes, the assumed enemy) rather than trying to muscle in and take ownership of their existing professional arena.

Territory VI: Collaborative Urbanism

'Designing a dream city is easy, rebuilding a living one takes imagination.'

Jane Jacobs[25]

From tactical urbanism to guerrilla pop-ups and community gardens, the 'bottoms up' movement has recently taken off. A territory that denies the big-wig designer for the solidarity of the individual, reclaiming their cities in a state of crisis.

The premise of this territory has great potential by shifting invention to the masses. The concern is that it falls prey to the economies of consumer greenwash[26] rather than social impact and actual change. This territory also suffers from the post-modern selfishness of the individual and NIMBYism, along with the multifaceted challenges associated with open source design.[27] The in-vogue notions that 'urban agriculture' will somehow save us is becoming a noxious rhetoric. Green walls, hipster container bars and 'green' apartments will not provide the innovative design solutions for future cities. With that said, the solidarity, adaptability and open source qualities that this territory affords, presents imperative solutions which must be fostered in pushing practice in a new direction.

Territory VII: Infrastructure Urbanism

'If we can change our assumptions about what infrastructure is then we can continue to experiment with what it might be yet...'

Jesse LeCavelleir[28]

Departing from the naturalistic ideals still manifest in previous territories, Infrastructure Urbanism reconsiders the very essence of 'the natural', by seeing our environments as inherently 'urban by nature'.[29] In this territory, landscape is rejected as a natural entity and seen through its conditioning as anthropogenic infrastructure. From 'Landscape Futures'[30] to 'Infrastructure as Architecture',[31] this territory is growing as we look beyond the green to the gritty realities of global extremities, crisis and disaster. This territory sees the beauty in the calamity of our infrastructural world (perhaps romanticised too much). The machine form aesthetic of Archigram, Iakov Chernikov and Lebbeus Woods. The Blade Runner dystopia against the potential for alternative modes of production. This territory presents a multi-disciplinary understanding of the complexities of our anthropogenic world and moves beyond glossy aesthetics to seeking innovative design solutions to global problems.

Territory VIII: Neo-Infrastructural

'Everything needs to be redesigned...'

Bruce Mau[32]

We are the accident.

The neo infrastructural represents a critical shift from the territories of the Hyper Civic to the territories of the Global Conduit. It does not manifest in isolation, but considers aspects of territories V–VII. The Neo Infrastructural denies the sublime, McHargian naturalisation, the post industrial and destination environments. The world is the invention, and we are its endemic accidents. The neo infrastructural is the subsequent invention of our accident. Continual, absolute, experimental. The Neo-Infrastructural is the technium,[33] the planetary urban,[34] the formal and the informal. It is not landscape, but surface, technology and flows, embedded and encountered. It is multiplicity, the ugly, the everyday, the crisis. It is not sustainable, it is resilient. It is the super-mega infrastructure (soft and hard), illegal and impossible. The everywhere (site) but nowhere (sight). It is anti-design, but all types of territory. It is anti-aesthetic, but with aesthetic.

Collaborative Urbanism:
View of Citizen 'Green'.
(Image by the author, May 2016, after Panini, View of the Roman Forum, c. 1747)

19. Ibid, 10, p. 177

20. For an overview of Heterotopias see: Foucault, M. (1967) Des Espace Aurtes translated in; Miskowiec, J (1884) Of Other Spaces: Utopias and Heterotopias Architecture/Mouvement/Continuité, October, pp. 2-9.

21. Post-Industrial has become a commonplace narrative in the landscape repertoire. From the original Latz Partners Duisburg Nord to McGregor Coxall's Ballast Point park Sydney. See landezine.com/post+industrial for lots of examples.

22. Berger, A. (2006). Drosscape. Landscape Urbanism Reader. p.209.

23. I.e. James Corner, Alan Berger, Charles Waldheim among others and the renowned Landscape Urbanism Reader (2006).

24. Ibid 22. after the concepts of 'stim' and 'dross' originally proposed by Lerup in; Lerup, L. (1995). Stim & Dross: Rethinking the Metropolis Assemblage, MIT Press, No. 25, Dec, pp. 82-101.

25. Jacobs, J. (1958, 2011) Downtown is for People, Fortune Magazine, September 18. Retrieved from http://fortune.com/2011/09/18/downtown-is-for-people-fortune-classic-1958/

26. For example recent designer apartments such as the Nightingale/ Assemble's Rossmoyne St which use the 'sustainable'/ 'open source'/ 'community' narrative by way of selling an inherently elitist product (not sustainability). E.g. see http://www.nightingale.melbourne/ [or] http://assembleprojects.com.au/projects/assemble-project/122-roseneath-st/

27. A good account of the challenges faced in this kind of approach is in: Ratti, C. (2015). Open Source Architecture, Thames & Hudson, London.

28. LeCavalier, J. (2010) Let's Infratecture!, in, Stoll, K & Lloyd S, eds., Infrastructure as Architecture: Designing Composite Networks, Jovis Verlag GMBH, Berlin, p. 111.

29. Sijmonds, J (2013) IABR 2014, An Introduction to Urban By Nature, IABR, Rotterdam.

30. See Manaugh, G (ed. 2013) Landscape Futures: Instruments Devices and Architectural Inventions, Actar, New York.

Neo-Infrastructural:
Landscape with Chaos in Flight
to the Unknown.
(Image by the author, May 2016, after Lorrain, Landscape with Rest in Flight to Egypt, c. 1647)

It is anti-consumption, but 100 per cent consuming. It is the share economy, the 99 per cent, the self-service myopia. It is not a dystopia. It is not a Utopia. It is a Foucauldian temporal heterotopia.[35] It is not static. It is continual. Adaptable. In flux. It is chaos, flight and a redefinition of practice as we know it.

Conclusion:

'Dystopia is old hat.'

Darryl Chen.[36]

This article sees territory as a multifaceted combination of accidents grouped and presented within an expanded field of practice. By journeying through the various territories, it argues we must critically shift beyond the representational imperative of the hyper civic (I–VI) and move to the informal, chaotic and resilient territories of the Neo Infrastructural.

Landscape has, for too long, been caught up in its own self-indulgent torpor. It's time to get critical. The Neo-Infrastructural may not be the answer; however, it is a starting point from which to abandon outdated, outmoded and obsolete territories of landscape. We must now move towards real agendas that deny aesthetic commodities in order to critically engage with the imminent challenges that are facing our world.

As Bruce Mau eloquently states: 'It's not about the world of design, but the design of the world.'[37]

31. See Stoll, K & Lloyd S (eds. 2010), Infrastructure as Architecture: Designing Composite Networks.

32. Mau, B (2004). Massive Change and the Institute Without Boundaries, Phaidon Press Limited, New York, p.15.

33. The technium is a poignant concept from Kevin Kelly considering technology as an extension of life (among other things), see for example: Kelly, K. (2010). What Technology Wants, Penguin Group, New York pp. 1-17.

34. For more on planetary urbanism and many more forward thinking critical ideas, see work by Neil Brenner. An excellent read is: Brenner, N & Schmid, C (2015) Towards a new epistemology of the Urban, City, Vol. 19, No. 2-3, pp. 151-182

35. ibid, 20.

36. Darryl Chen speaking at the Failed Architecture Conference, FA# 10 (2013) Beyond Failure. Accessed March 2014, watch online at http://www.failedarchitecture.com/fa10-beyond-failure/

37. ibid, 32.

FRANCE(S) TERRITOIRE LIQUIDE

PAUL WOMBELL

Upon the fall of the Berlin Wall in 1989 and the enlargement of the European Union (EU) - now with 28 member states - the borders of national states within the EU have become permeable with the free movement of citizens and goods. New developments in transportation such as high-speed trains and short-haul air flights have made travel easy and inexpensive. Developments in telecommunications have made receiving and sending information instantaneous, both within the nation state, but also globally. The World Wide Web, home computers and digital technologies have changed the nature of photography, both in the making of images and their distribution. These changes raise questions about where the boundary of the nation starts and ends, how the landscape has been transformed by these changes, where photographers locate themselves to take photographs of this fluid landscape, and whether these changes undermine what it means to be a citizen of any nation?

Over the last 25 years different nation states within the EU have supported photographic projects that have prompted the idea of the unified European state. These cultural initiatives have generally coincided with the enlargement of the EU.

In early 2011 a group of photographers started to discuss the idea of a new mission that would pictorially redefine the territory of France at the beginning of the twenty-first century. Over time the group increased to over 50 photographers. Originally working under the title 'WAF: The Mission on the New French Landscape', this was changed in late 2012 to 'France(s) Territoire Liquide'.[1] The metaphor liquid was a reference to the writings of Zygmunt Bauman and his use of liquid modernity as a term to describe the condition of constant mobility, fragility in relationships and constantly changing identities that form part of our daily life within contemporary society.

The photographers involved with the Mission produced work that tracked the malleable boundaries between analog and digital photography, between the uncertain boundaries between reality and fiction and the vanishing boundaries of France. In a simple way, they are asking what does it mean to be French at the beginning of the twenty-first century? What does France look like? How might photography represent the territory of the nation? But more importantly, they are asking, does France exist?

Frédéric Delangle

Frédéric Delangle's project starts with large black and white photographs that he took at road junctions in Paris. They are without any dramatic visual interest, with a certain quality of detachment and flatness. But this is the beginning of an interesting journey that will bring a different form of life to the streets of Paris. One of the key elements of globalisation is the outsourcing of business procedures to other parts of the world, in particular Asia. Delangle sent his photographic prints to India where skilled painters printed over the print by adding streets advertisements that make reference to Indian culture and commerce. The result is colonisation of the French urban landscape by the Hindi language. A new hybrid location is formed on the surface of the photographic print, the amalgamation of two cultures that creates Paridelhi.

From left to top right:
Paris Delhi 1
P-D Stalingrad 2014
Canal Bastille

From top to bottom right:
Altitude 1780
Altitude 2330
Altitude 1520

Emmanuelle Blanc

The main features in Emmanuelle Blanc's photographs taken in the northern region of the French Alps are the forests, waterfalls and the exposed sedimentary rock strata. Each stratum is made up of different material deposits that have been formed over one million years. However if you look more closely you will find signs of more recent additions: electrical power pylons and electrical cables that transect the terrain. The French electrical transmission system is the largest in Europe and interconnects to its neighbouring countries as a member of the synchronous grid system of Continental Europe. This grid supplies electrical power across national boarders to 24 countries. Blanc's photographs suggest in a subtle way that the Alps have their own kind of power and own time frame beyond the transitory nature of human time and that humans will eventually become just one more stratum within the rock formation.

Yann De Fareins

At first glance, the photographs of Yann de Fareins might not seem to have any relationship to the issues of power and revolution. However, these photographs of minor roads in the department of Gard in the Languedoc-Roussillon-Midi-Pyrénées region of southern France trace the shifting history of political power. The subtle changes to the road surface due to repairs or the forlorn kilometre stone markers at the side of the road signify the administrative boundaries between various parishes that were originally created on 4 March 1790. These traces represent the re-ordering of political space that took place in the late eighteenth century due to the French Revolution with the abolition of the monarchy and the formation of the Republic.

1. 'France(s) Territoire Liquide' consists of 43 participating photographers. To view the work of all the photographers visit http://www.francesterritoireliquide.fr/

Les Arpe nteurs

Anne Favret and Patrick Manez

Anne Favret and Patrick Manez's photographs of a rocky terrain with strange shaped buildings give the impression that this could be a terrain from another planet. Yet this is the location of the Centre d'Etudes et de Recherches Géodynamiques et Astronomiques observatory that is situated on the Calern Plateau just north of Nice. With a team of technicians and scientists working on the development and manufacturing of scientific instruments such as telescopes and lasers, the observatory studies stars and objects in the universe, the movement of tectonic plates on earth, and tests theories such as Einstein's theory of relativity. From this location the scientists seek out life on other planets, measure the movement of the earth's crust, and test the liquidity of space and time.

Albin Millot

With the integration of many countries into the European Union, the nation state is witnessing a fundamental challenge to its status. Territorial integrity has been superseded by shared sovereignty and the interconnection of interests with power transferred to trans-European institutions. This can be seen clearly in the Schengen Agreement of 1995 that abolished internal border controls to assist the free movement of people between most countries in the European Union. Millot's project was to seek out the now disappearing national boundary of France. He travelled to the borders that France shares with six other countries to find where the nations once met each other. To define what can't be seen, he marked out the boundary between the different countries with lights sticks. The result is a photographic depiction of the disappearing boundary of France.

Top left:
France/Belgique/Luxembourg - 49°32'46.94_N 5°49'6.67_E

Top right:
France _ Suisse _ Italie - 45°55'21.24_N 7° 2'39.82_E

Bottom left:
Point Extrême Ouest - Pointe de Corsen, Plouarzel, Finistère - 48°24'46.87_N 4°47'42.46_O

Emilie Vialet

Emilie Vialet's photographic project depicts the southern western coastal zone of France that forms part of the Bay of Biscay. The coastline is flat with long beaches, sand dunes and marshlands, which are exposed to westerly winds and tidal currents. Les Landes as the region is known, was once an expansive pine forest that was destroyed in 407 CE by the Vandals, who razed the villages and set fire to the forests, destroying the cover of this vast sandy area. With the prevailing winds thus began the movement of sand from the coast into the hinterland that dammed streams, causing marshlands to form. In the late eighteenth century Napoleon appointed the engineer Nicolas Brémontier to construct a dike to stop the movement of the sand. Today it is still a constant battle to control the moving sand dunes, forming the subject of Emilie Vialet's project.

La Lette

(Project)

TWO GEOSTORIES
Design Earth

'Belly of a Mountain' and 'A Geographic Stroll Around the Horizon' are early projects from the 'Geostories' series by DESIGN EARTH. In an epoch that is defined by climate risks and resource territories at the scale of the planet, 'Geostories' outlines a manifesto on the environmental imagination through the medium of the architectural project. The prefix Geo- engages the Earth as a grand question of design making formal the unaccounted for spaces of environmental externalities. The suffix -stories channels such matters, which are difficult both to tell and to hear, into geographic fictions on technological systems.

Belly of a Mountain

The mountains of Sugarloaf, Corcovado and a profile of hills around Guanabara Bay have physically and symbolically marked the Carioca landscapes. The urbanisation of Rio de Janeiro, however, and in particular the growth of its urban infrastructures, such as energy facilities, logistic zones, landfills, and processing industries, are butting up against the mountain ranges and putting pressure on the city's geographical contours. The city plans to relocate such urban programs outside of the city to clear valuable real estate for future development, all while preserving the Tijuca Forest National Park that hosts the colossal sculpture of Christ the Redeemer atop Corcovado Mountain.

Such an attitude divides landscapes into land too pure to be used, and land so defiled with waste that it must be extradited. The project articulates a position against such isolation of green and grey natures into two distinct spheres, one the preservation of a landform into a World Heritage cultural landscape and the second the displacement and burial of other landscapes below a green carpet, or what we refer to as landfill. It is a critique of an urbanism focused on the metropolis and an ecology concerned with a preserved nature.

'Belly of a Mountain' reacts to such an organisation of space by collapsing the space of the nature reserve and that of the toxic zone: it is a site of both sanctification and defilement. The project preserves the formal green shell of the iconic Corcovado all while incorporating banished externalities in a series of excavated mountain grottos at the site of such an iconic landform. The Mountain takes in the cemeteries, water purification plants and other facilities. By assembling aberrations, it draws us into to the shadowy nature of the Earth and of our humanity, and through that aspires to reconfigure the aesthetic and organisational assumptions upon which the totality of urbanisation rests.

A Geographic Stroll Around the Horizon

'We have an even bigger horizon ahead of us', notes the major Brazilian oil company on its website after the 2007 discovery of mega-fields in the South Atlantic. Opening up the petroleum horizon, the offshore oil basins have constituted a new province within 183 kilometres of the coast of Rio. Although such territory is inscribed in an extensive network of oil blocks, transportation vectors, drilling axes and labour nodes, the image of the offshore horizon is singularly identified with that of the rig perpetuating an urban imaginary of zones of exception, of isolated platforms beyond environmental and economic accountability.

'A Geographic Stroll Around the Horizon' counters the abstraction of the sea into a logistical zone by expanding the spatial and cognitive imaginary of the city of Rio de Janeiro to its ocean-hinterland. The project draws on the horizon as a geographic aesthetic that renders legible the offshore territorial project. Set at a distance of 4.7 kilometres for an observer standing on the Earth's surface, the distance to the visible horizon at sea has been important as it represented the range of communication, vision and knowledge.

A Geographic Stroll Around the Horizon

Following page: Belly of a Mountain

Atlantic Ocean
Sambadrom Marques de Sapucai

748
534
493
458
407
343
251
166
70
0
PPPPPP

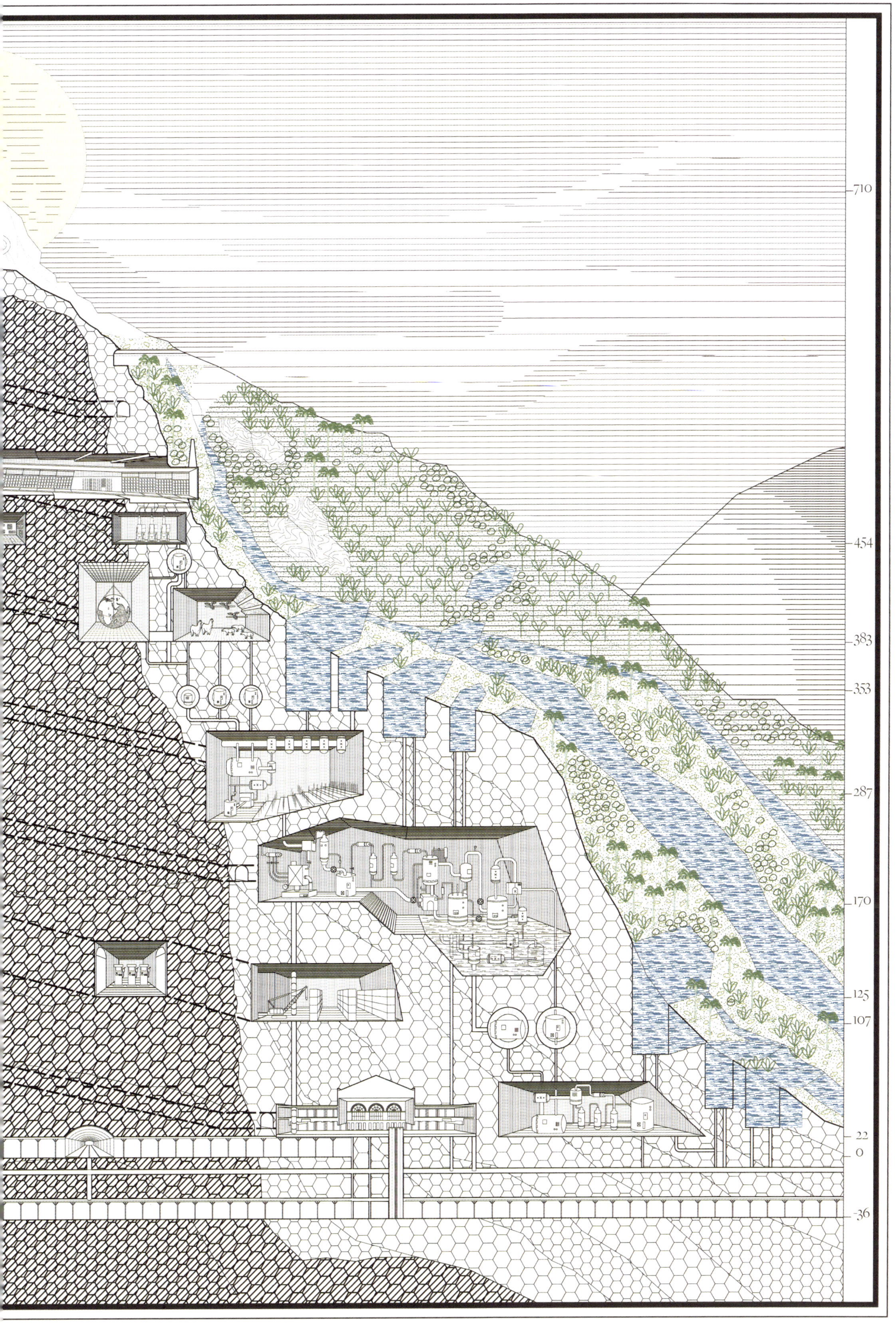
710
454
383
353
287
170
125
107
22
0
-36

UNDER THE SEA THERE IS A HOLE

COOKING SECTIONS

Since the early 2000s, landmasses have been collapsing around the Dead Sea at an ever-increasing rate. These sinkholes have taken over the unique desert, with over 4000 documented holes, some as large as 2 kilometres long and 25 metres deep. The phenomenon is linked to the depletion of the Dead Sea and the rapid drop in sea level, more than a metre per year. Water runoff from the desertified mountains seeps into the ground where the sea once lay; it dissolves the underground deposits of rock salt and creates huge cavities that eventually surrender to the weight of the earth on top. Driving along the banks of the Dead Sea, the sight of abandoned beach resorts, empty buildings and diverted roads amidst the arid landscape feels like an apocalypse in the lowest place on earth. Three main forces are accountable for this radical transformation that is making the surface of the Earth float above caverns: a series of dams built along the Jordan River basin in Israel, Jordan, Syria and Lebanon; the appropriation and exhaustion of underground water resources by Israeli date palm plantations in the Occupied Palestinian Territories; and above all the extraction of minerals for the production of fertilisers from the evaporation ponds run by the Dead Sea Works in Israel and the Arab Potash Company in Jordan. These dining tables map out the imminent risk zone along the Dead Sea shoreline and the geological transformations that have occurred to it. The unstable surfaces serve as the basis to discuss together the challenges around destroying landscapes in order to feed the world.

While the fossil fuel industry often seems like the worst perpetrator of climate change, the activity most rapidly transforming the planet is in fact the 'misuse of land'. Many studies have proven how eating less meat would have an unprecedented impact on the acceleration of climate change, but how do other food choices we make harm the landscape? How can we re-shape space through our eating habits? Citizens of the global North generally underestimate the direct impact of dietary choices on the landscape, and especially on climate change. Local and organic foods are more marketable than ever, yet their impact on the environment is slow, possibly even negligible. If our eating habits have such a significant impact on climate change, then there is an urgent need to bring eaters and policymakers to the dining table.

CLIMAVORE is a performative dinner that aims to consider a diet based on new climatic seasons. Different from the now obsolete cycle of spring, summer, autumn, and winter, they react to current drought, desertification, water pollution, flash floods, and invasion of species. These seasons offer a new set of clues about how to adapt our diet to the needs of global landscape. In a severe drought, eating tomatoes that are local and organic can still be environmentally destructive. Instead, CLIMAVORE aims to develop a diet that does not just 'do harm', but uses diet as a means of rehabilitating and re-imagining agriculture production. Eating invasive species limits their population growth, eating nitrogen-fixing plants can restore the soil; one adult mussel can filter as much as 40 litres of water per day. The urgency to speculate about these new scenarios approaches food as an infrastructural means to rebuild environments.

Invasive Season

The Plant That Could Sink Your Mortgage Cordial

Gin & Japanese Knotweed

Alien Waters Gin & Ground Elder

The operating of the Suez Canal in 1869 developed by French diplomat Ferdinand de Lesseps generated an unprecedented man-induced migration of fish. Known as the Lessepsian Migration, this phenomenon describes how Red Sea species 'invaded' the more nutritious Mediterranean waters through the newly created passage. In an age of extreme containerisation, shipping and exchange of ballast waters across different oceans, we are assisting a series of species to spread across far away territories that are being turned into civilian enemies for

the 'nation'. Countries like the Cayman Islands are fighting the annihilation of their local marine diversity by turning invasive lionfish into a national dish. In a climavore diet we would have to eat invasive species for a certain amount of years until the environmental hazard they constitute disappears. The ultimate goal of a restaurant serving invasive species is to go bankrupt.

Forever Fertile Season

Nitrogen Fixation Mulch Alfalfa, Buckwheat, Peas

Today the earth is capable of producing almost anything anytime by making soil constantly fertile. However, the mineral extraction behind the production of fertilisers has destroyed landscapes in the name of solving the world's hunger. Possible alternatives could either be to increase the use of organic compost or decrease chemical products. Some crops have been proven to capture nitrogen from the air and naturally fixate it to the soil while growing in rotational cycles.

Drought Season

Water Stress Salad Lentils, Millet, Pomegranate, Carob, Pepper, Thyme

Different regions are transnationally struck by heat waves and cycles of drought that can last for several years. Recently we have seen the fertile state of California suffering the consequences of excessive irrigation. In times of water scarcity crops requiring less irrigation could be planted to contribute to the exhaustion of aquifers. The technique of growing vegetables under water stress has even been proven in some places to enhance the flavour of the resulting green.

Flash Flood Season

Brackish Agricultures Sea-lavender, Elderberry, Beets

Intensive agriculture and inappropriate irrigation methods are decreasing freshwater supplies. This makes soils become more and more saline due to sea level rise in coastal flat lands or the current increase in flash floods. Saline crops can constitute the future of a brackish form of agriculture reshaping coastal landscapes under threat: seaside vegetables that are highly salt-tolerant; sea kale or elderberry that retain the ground in case of a sudden flood while quickly absorbing water; and new species thriving in these new landscapes, such as Dutch saltwater-grown potatoes or English saltmarsh lamb that grazes by the sea.

Ocean Cleaning Season

Floating Purifiers mussels, Kelp, Wakame

Being the single shoreless sea in the planet, the Sargasso Sea lays in the Atlantic Ocean 1500 kilometres away from the coast of Florida. Blooms of Sargassum Seaweed are nonetheless reaching the coasts of Caribbean resorts making the beaches impracticable, as new reserves of seaweed are forming along the North Equatorial Counter Current due to anthropogenic action. This new blooming site, drifting onto the shores of Caribbean and West African countries, affect both tourist and fishing industries that are fundamental for local economies. Could Sargasso Seaweed become a frequent edible, profitable enough to incentivise the cleaning of the shores? Seaweeds, kelp and some bivalve crustaceans like mussels, oyster and clams are crucial agents in purifying coastal seawater from pollutants, while constituting a food source without need of irrigation.

Desertification Season

Desert Stoppers Moringa

One of the spaces with incomparable potential for the development of another understanding of ecology is the Sahara Desert. Despite having been described as an ungovernable landscape, the edge of the desert (the Sahel) is a region spanning over 7000 kilometres from the west to the east coasts of the African continent that can shed a light on how to deal with nature and urbanity in a postcolonial context. In 2010 a pan-African alliance of the eleven countries along the edge of the Sahara (PAGGW) committed to one of the most relevant agro-engineering projects of the twenty-first century: the construction of a Great Green Wall to slow down desertification at a transnational level. This ten-mile afforestation project consist of drought-resistant species requiring little irrigation, ranging from gum trees to moringa trees.

(Project)

A CARTOGRAPHIC AND POLITICAL ENQUIRY ON BORDERS AND CLIMATE CHANGE

Italian Limes

Installation of the border measurement devices on the Grafferner glacier in the Ötztal Alps, Austrian-Italian border, April 2016. Landscape view of the sensors' grid installed on the ice sheet, across the Alpine watershed.

Installation of the border measurement devices on the Grafferner glacier in the Ötztal Alps, Austrian-Italian border, April 2016. Besides Italian Limes' team, the expedition's members included representatives from the Italian Glaciological Committee, geophysicists from the National Institute of Oceanography and Experimental Geophysics, glaciologists from the University of Padua and Parma and journalist Livia Albeck-Ripka.

Measuring a Nation

Italy's terrestrial border unwinds for a total length of 1,913 kilometres, mostly following the line of the natural watershed across the Alps. On rocky ridges and stable terrains, its contour is materialised through 8,043 boundary stones and metal plaques. On the snowfields and perennial glaciers that shape the watershed at higher altitudes, where permanent physical markers would be impossible, the only trace of the border is preserved in the official maps published by Istituto Geografico Militare, Italy's national mapping agency.

The current border geography was mostly defined by the Treaty of Peace signed by Italy in 1947, after the end of the Second World War, and its short history since then reflects many of the political developments in modern Europe. After the stipulation of the Schengen Agreements in 1985, the border seemed to tangibly fade away, following the disappearance of the architectural outposts that signaled passport controls on every main Alpine crossing.

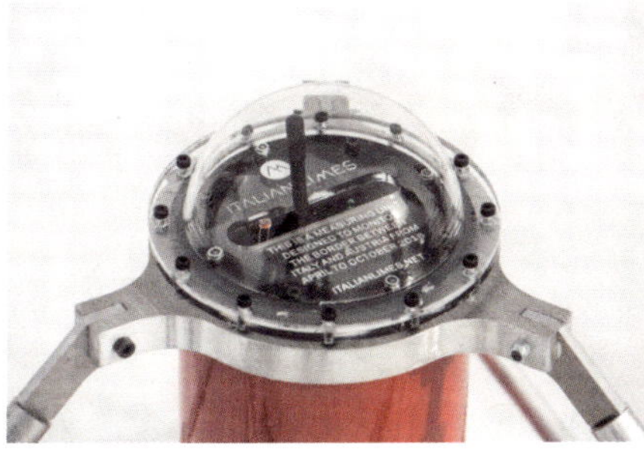

Installation of the border measurement devices on the Grafferner glacier in the Ötztal Alps, Austrian-Italian border, April 2016. Detail of one of the 25 sensors installed on the ice sheet.

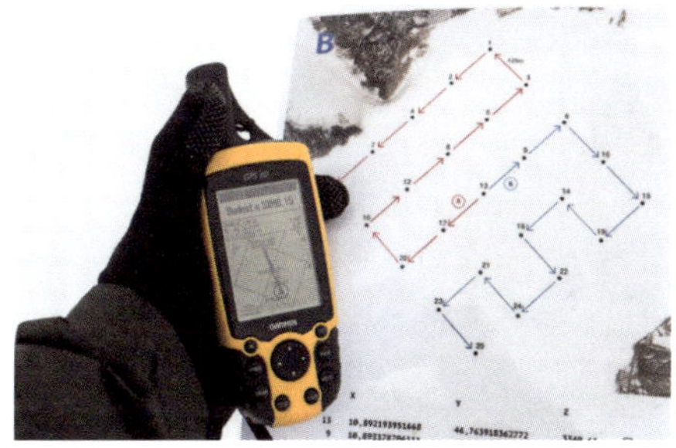

Installation of the border measurement devices on the Grafferner glacier in the Ötztal Alps, Austrian-Italian border, April 2016. Definition of the sensors' grid across the watershed.

Installation of the border measurement devices on the Grafferner glacier in the Ötztal Alps, Austrian-Italian border, April 2016. Landscape view of one of the 25 sensors installed on the ice sheet.

Melting Glaciers

Since 1850, Alpine glaciers have experienced a 50 per cent decrease in their overall extension. Cyclical variations of the ice surface have accumulated into permanent shifts and alterations of the glacier geography, causing significant drifts of the watershed line and, as a result, the coinciding national borders. As a consequence of the progressive retreat of the glaciers, the Alpine watershed has undergone considerable displacements in recent years, making it necessary to renegotiate the terms of the boundary between Italy and its neighbouring countries. The watershed is often difficult to discern on the territory, as it can correspond to different elements – such as mountain ridges, passes, valley floors, wetlands or underground culverts. As a continuous, uninterrupted line, it therefore exists primarily on a map, rather than being an indisputable element of mountain topography.

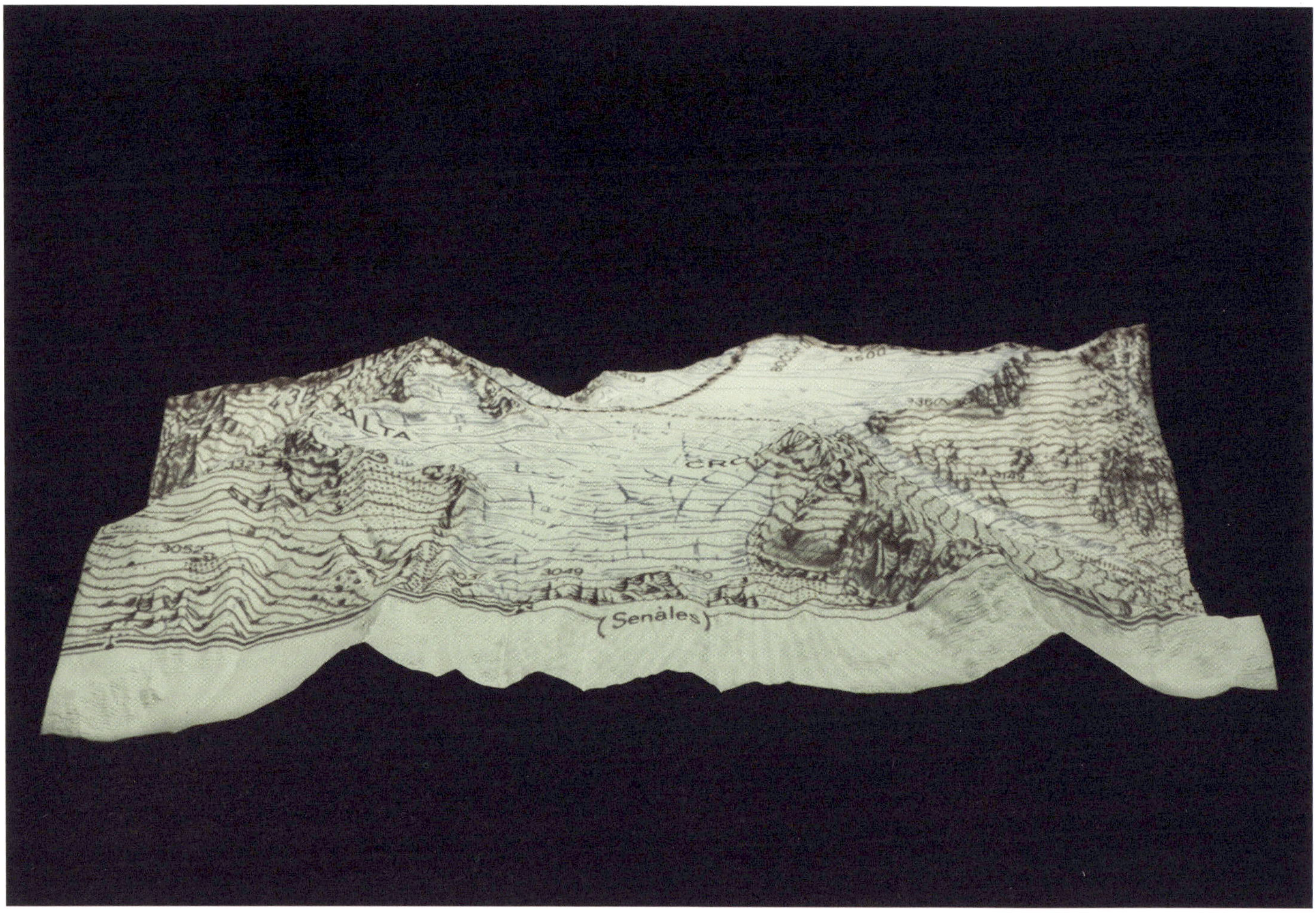
3052
3049
(Senàles)

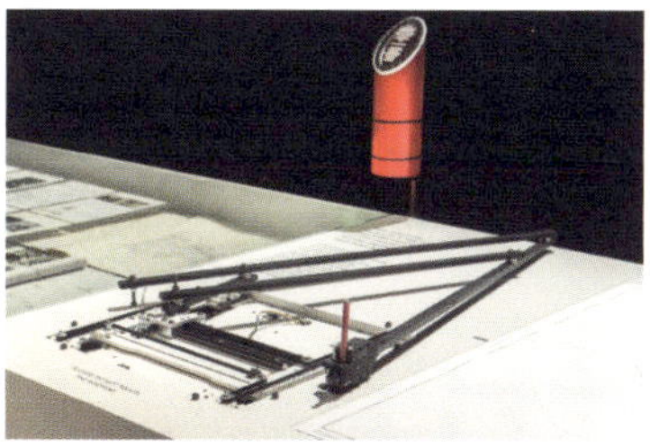

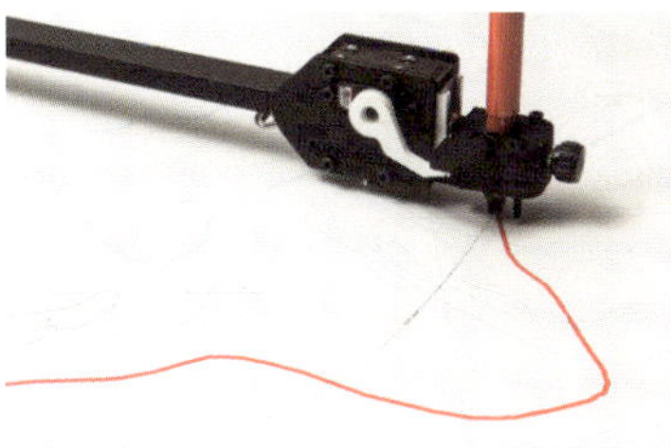

Detailed view of the interactive installation (drawing machine).

General view of the interactive installation.

Left:
Detailed view of the interactive installation (raised-relief model).

Automated Drawing

Since 2014, when Italian Limes started to monitor the shifts in the Austrian/Italian watershed, international borders have become one of the most reported topics on public media. A network of apparently dormant nineteenth century border checks woke up from the dream of a borderless continent and materialised into a twenty-first century psychosis of police checks, barbed wire fences, migrant encampments, proxy sovereignties and displaced jurisdictions. Schengen's Europe is on the verge of a total collapse, in a way nobody imagined when the project first looked at the invisible lines that lay high on the glaciers, and that once seemed the perfect representation for this vanishing infrastructure of coordinates and boundary stones. Almost completely exiled into the map, borders have claimed back their mark into the territory, wielded by the governments as the ultimate defense for the continuance of the nation state. Over the course of spring and summer 2016, a grid of autonomous devices installed on a melting ice sheet across the Austrian/Italian border will track this moveable frontier, in order to visualise in real time its daily infinitesimal shifts. The measuring units are solarpowered devices that have been designed to record precise altitude measurements and a series of other environmental data, useful to understand their location and the weather conditions on the glacier. Their data are processed remotely in order to monitor any change in the glacier surface, detecting in real time the evolution of the watershed geography. A drawing machine, exhibited at ZKM in Karlsruhe as part of the 'Reset Modernity!' exhibition curated by Bruno Latour, will print on demand maps of the moving border, each of them time stamped on the exact moment of a person visits the installation.

- Marco Ferrari

Italian Limes is a project by Folder (Marco Ferrari, Elisa Pasqual), Delfino Sisto Legnani, Pietro Leoni, Alessandro Mason, Angelo Semeraro and Livia Shamir.

Image Credits:
Delfino Sisto Legnani

BEN BUTLER

Unbounded Statement (Emergence)

Every thing, under close enough observation, will reveal the complete story of its making.

In and around Blue Hill, Maine, the blueberry fields are littered with the stones, boulders really, which were dropped by migrating glaciers during the last ice age. They are not indigenous like the bedrock, they are visitors, and they generally sit on top of the earth.

Stones can seem like the most static and permanent objects we can imagine, but of course they are not static. Time spent with these particular rocks shows clear evidence of multiple processes – cracks where an enormous force once suddenly split the rock, concavities where a violent encounter with another stone took a small part away, a surface texture resulting from centuries of abrasion from ice and soil and smaller rocks, and a general smoothness, a softening of all features, from the gentle but endlessly persistent wind and rain. In the quiet of the blueberry fields you can study these features and reconstruct the story. A single stone was severed from a mountain, tumbled, was tossed about by heaving earth, carried across a continent by flowing ice, scraped and sculpted, and ended up here. And it is still moving, sinking into the soil, shifting upward and tilting when the ground freezes, softening in the rain, cracking, and rolling down hill, all at pace that is difficult to perceive. But the physical evidence is there in the stone.

My sculptures reflect the sensibility that an object stands as a momentary physical manifestation of an ongoing process. They provide evidence of unseen forces, and they point to the distinction between the human and the non-human. Humans design complexity, whereas in nature it emerges without design, but instead through simple and persistent accumulation. When the order of things is not readily apparent, complexity is often mistaken for chaos. In the rush to comprehend we often miss the wonderful unseen forces at work.

My response is to play in these boundaries between the simple and the complex, and between the complex and the overwhelming.

I am fascinated by complex phenomena that emerge from very simple processes. This is the underlying behavior of the natural world, and vivid examples can be found at every scale. Biology emerges from chemistry. The experience of consciousness emerges from the accumulation of neural activity. The myriad activities and complex behaviors observed in ant colonies, and even human cites, are simply the product of the accumulation of the myopic actions of individuals within those societies. Unbounded, my installation at Rice Gallery, is essentially a distillation of this idea. Simple and predictable units are accumulated until an unexpectedly rich range of physical and visual phenomena emerge.

Photo credits:
Nash Baker

MEDIATION MEDIATION EDIATION

MEDIATION MEDIATION MED

MEDI ION ME ATI ED

M ATION M A N MEDIA N DIATION D

ON ATI D

D

MEDIATION MEDIATION MEDIATIO

D

M ATION ED

MEDIATION

ON AT D

D

MEDIA ED ION ME AT MEDIA

ED IO MEDIATIO

MEDIATION DIATION MED

ED NI ATI ED

M ATION MEDI ON M ATIO MEDI ON

MEDIATION

MEDIATION MEDIATION MEDIATION

TION MEDIATION MEDIATION

T I

TIC EDIA ON MEI ATION

T I O

TI MEDIAT M IATION M IA N MEDIA ON

TI N MEDIATION MEDIATION

TI

TION MEDI ION

TI M IA ON

ME ATION EDIA ON MF ATIO MEDIA ON

TI DI MI

EDIATION MEDIATION MEDIATION

TI

TIC MEDIA ON

MEDIATION

TI DI ON ML ATION

T I

M ATION DI ON MEL TIC MEDIA N

EDIATION MEDIATION MEDIATION MEDIATION MEDIATIO

TION MEDIAT N MED ION

TI MEDIATION ED ION MEDIA N N ATIONME TI

ME ATION EDIA ON MF ATIO MEDIA ON

MEDIATION

Olafur Eliasson

:

REPOSITIONED TERRITORIES

Olafur Eliasson's varied works of art are inspired by challenges our world faces. Kerb explores two of his pieces, discussing their poignant representations of territorial entwinement and the potential for landscape architecture to take up his call to action.

Eliasson's Ice Watch declares that humans are a force of nature; as such we make large contributions to the future of the planet. These are not necessarily new statements but their consideration by Eliasson in Ice Watch compels further action. Through a method Kerb terms territorial repositioning, chunks of free floating glacial ice were transported and placed in an urban context, successfully isolating a foreign territory to show a distinct correlation between urban progress and climate fuelled environmental degradation.

This high profile piece aimed to have its message heard by the widest variety of people possible. Unveiled at the COP21 United Nations Conference on Climate Change in Paris 2015, it was openly accessible to public and global leaders alike. However even with such grand exposure it begs the question: who will take up Ice Watch's call to action? In a perfect world one might think that both community and different scales of governance would join together in direct action to understand and address issues that the piece raises. Perhaps a more powerful stance is that the onus

1. Chambers, R. (2012): Participation for development: A good time to be alive - Devpolicy Blog from the development policy centre. Aid effectiveness. Devpolicy Blog from the Development Policy Centre Retrieved from http://webcache.googleusercontent.com/search?q=cache:0ZIGZHr4qioJ:devpolicy.org/participation-for-development-a-good-time-to-be-alive-20121207-2/+&cd=1&hl=en&ct=clnk&gl=au.

Ice Watch
Project by Olafur Eliasson and Minik Rosing
Date: 2014-2015
Location: City Hall Square Copenhagen and Place du Panthéon, Paris

Photography by Martin Argyroglo

is on each individual to delve into what they understand, that each one of us can make a difference, and on a daily and hourly basis. Many big changes come from many small actions of many, many people.[1] With this notion in mind it is pertinent to explore how design minds can make a contribution.

Ice Watch is contextualised by climatic history. The ice contained in the Antarctic and Greenland sheets formed through hundreds of thousands of years of accumulated snow, compacted into glacial ice under its own weight. Glacial ice is made up of visible layers, each a snapshot of the snow that fell during a given year. Likewise, the bubbles trapped in the ice contain samples of the atmosphere as it was at the time the snow fell. Ice contains memories of how the climate and the atmosphere have changed over hundreds of millennia.[2] Additionally, Eliasson's visceral, experiential narrative of a trip to the Arctic, cements the piece's relevance. 'I have a very lively memory of the horrifying noise and sight of huge ice blocks cracking and breaking away from the pack'.[3] Territorial terms can

clarify the importance of context. The context of any design project can be considered the container or the 'border' for the piece. Responding to existing context can enable design to manipulate boundaries with specific goals.

Eliasson exhibited Riverbed at the Danish Louisiana Museum of Modern Art. When talking about his experience of this work Eliasson said it evoked contemplations of what reality is.

He states, 'The way we take in the world is not natural, it's cultural'. For each individual experiencing this installation, 'the authorship of reality lies within the beholder and the museum is constituted by the visitor'.[4]

Applying this rationale to any territory we exist in, transition through or aim to impact can throw up a myriad of ideas applicable to design. An idea worth testing might be the impact of cultural norms on the creation of existing

2. Eliasson, Olafur and Rosing, Minik (2015): Ice, Art, and Being Human. Retrived from http://icewatchparis.com/.

3. ibid

4. Louisiana Channel (2014): Olafur Eliasson: A Riverbed inside the museum. YouTube. Retrieved from https://www.youtube.com/watch?v=ZLUX3AI2Uic.

Riverbed
Project by Olafur Eliasson
Date: 2014–2015
Location: Humlebæk Denmark

Photography by Anders Sune Berg

territories, and furthermore whether a specific landscape intervention would yield specific changes to appropriation of sites. Riverbed illustrates what occurs when a layer of landscape is separated from its norm, people were able to experience a river in a way that tests our preconceived notions of territory, breaking the boundaries of original context. Landscape architects are not alone in taking on the challenges of our changing world, however they are certainly called to take an active role in envisioning future landscapes for humanity. This being the case, their understanding of territorial connections and boundaries can become tools, especially pertinent in driving the design process as well as furthering collectivised action through interdisciplinary collaboration.

This piece was written by the Kerb Editors: Louella Exton, Millicent Gunner, Emma Groot, Hayden Matthys and Kim Morte.

STREETSCAPE TERRITORIES: A RESEARCH PROJECT

KRIS SCHEERLINCK

Streetscape Territories is the name given to a research project about the transformation of the urban fabric with a focus on the constant re-configuration of its streetscapes. The research deals with the way architectural artifacts, systems of open spaces, property structures and their inherent accessibility and permeability models configure streetscapes and how their inhabitants can read and give meaning to them.

This project focuses on accessibility and models of proximity within a street, neighbourhood or region and starts from the assumption that urban space, from the domestic scale to the scale of the city, can be understood as a discontinuous collective space,[1 2 3] containing different levels of shared use that are defined by multiple physical, cultural or territorial boundaries.[4] In this research project, urban space is not considered as unconditionally accessible by all users, as urbanity depends on giving as well as restricting access to territories, this way defining the identity of a place. As a consequence, urban space cannot - and should not - be characterised by overall continuity as it responds to mechanisms of providing and denying conditions for privacy or community. These mechanisms employ systems of borders and boundaries[5] to configure sets of aggregated, integrated or overlapped territories that are read, interpreted and used in multiple ways. The main research question of the project is: how do territories and people relate to each other and how do these relationships contribute to the local identity of the physical and social environment?

The intermediate scale,[6] that is the scale between the architectural intervention and the urbanistic plan, defines the research domain. Within this research project, collective spaces that are characterised by a 'between/among' space condition are read, mapped or designed; systems of streets, squares, gardens and parks, and also patios, porches, enclaves, covered or portico spaces, courtyards and all other interstitial areas are subject of research. The research consists of systematic and comparative analysis of existing neighborhoods, streetscapes, public spaces, urban landscapes or complex buildings in different locations, based on research by design. It includes multiple approaches from different disciplinary fields, and considers research and design as simultaneous and integrated processes of developing urban projects. The overarching aim of the research approach is to provide new research methods and insights to facilitate a critical and productive discussion on the transformation of the contemporary urban fabric, manifested through its multiple dynamic streetscapes.

The project focuses on the territorial organisation of streetscapes explored in different contexts, studied as part of different cultures and defined by different social networks. It starts with the assumption that streetscape is subject of constant negotiation and part of scenarios of uncertainty at different levels. Uncertainty is a very important dimension in planning a design process[7] as we do not have control over every single aspect of that process. Many elements remain unpredictable, unstable or even unknown in a political, environmental, social or economic way. Because of the multi-layered character of urban projects there is a certain complexity and non-linear process that often seems to overtake the overall urban development. For this reason, multiplicity, ambivalence and a lack of definition are always the starting point of the Streetscape Territories projects.

The research and design approaches are defined by five main concepts, described in the following part of this article.

Depth

According to N.J. Habraken,[8] the built environment, defined by territorial

organisation, is founded on the principle of inclusion within other territories. The author relates this very principle to the transition between private and public spaces. Imagining different accessibility patterns within this theoretical model of inclusion, that is, different ways of entering those territorial scenarios, N.J. Habraken defines in a clear way the concept of territorial depth. 'Territorial depth is measured by the number of boundary crossings...needed to move from the outer space to the innermost territory'.[9] However, territorial depth is not a static parameter: within a time framework, after the intervention of various urban agents, depth can increase or decrease, according to the specific characteristics and dynamics of the built environment.

Bill Hillier and Julienne Hanson[10] also refer to depth and describe how architecture structures the systems of space we inhabit and how those systems are related with a social life: movement, encounter of social relations or avoidance are part of architectural social vocabulary. Apart from theoretical models that deal with space without a social context or studies of society without a spatial context, they propose a new model to understand the built environment, starting from applied disciplines. First, this means that a social context of spatial patterning is studied with a simultaneous analysis of a spatial context of social patterning. Second, they suggest a new method of analysis of spatial patterns: one that concentrates on the relation between local morphologic relations and global patterns. This includes a theory of pattern types and a description of a method of analysis. Above all, they believe in the non-hierarchical, abstract notions of spatial relations between buildings or other elements, defining the environment. They point out that syntactic generators of space are shape-free: the study of space as a system is not about shape. Besides that, they dedicate a limited role to 'distances' or 'location' and focus on simultaneously existing relationships that are ever-changing. In other words, they are interested in rethinking the concept of proximity at an urban scale.

According to the authors, buildings define empty volumes of space in between, which can be seen as ordering space. They mention that buildings seem to be physical artifacts, but that this is illusionary: transformations of space through objects means ordering relations between people. In other words, this constitutes a system of social relations.

Bill Hillier[11] continues the analysis of space syntax and tries to define the concept of relations: '...relations, especially spatial relations are very puzzling entities...We must accept that... the relation, like the term it relates, is not dependent on thoughts, but belongs to the independent world which thought apprehends, but does not create.' This independent world is full of complex relational schemes, between areas, buildings, users, voids and program defined configurations. A configuration is:

"a set of relationships among things all of which interdepend in an overall structure of some kind...If we define spatial relations as existing when there is any type of link - say adjacency or permeability - between two spaces, then configuration exists when relations between two spaces are changed according to how we relate one or both to at least one other space"[12]

Collective Space

Processes of spatial specialisation and socio-functional segregation go together with increasing thematisation and extreme systematisation of the built environment, understood as live configurations.[13] These configurations are defined by the way the public realm is related to private spheres. Nevertheless, the traditional dichotomy of public versus private space loses strength as new models of space use and production arise. The recently mentioned spatial phenomena ask for a new understanding that is no more based on a division between private or public space but deals with collective use of space. In a way, Manuel de Solà-Morales questioned two aspects of the traditional definition of public space: that it should be publicly owned to have a collective dimension, and that it should be freely accessible by everyone. The author argues: 'It is a fact that the city is the very place where the private domain can be, and often is, a social domain - just as much as or indeed even more than the public domain...Private buildings as public elements, radiating social meaning and value that extend beyond the actual buildings embody their urban character'.[14] Tom Avermaete and Hans Teerds,[15] make a comparative study in 'Architectural Positions on the Public Sphere': '...to de Solà-Morales, both these attributes were becoming obsolete, and he argued that even in the most traditional European cities, much public life was developing elsewhere.' The very nature of the property, that is who owns the piece of land or the building, becomes less important than the way we use space. They continue saying that, as a response, Manuel de Solà-Morales suggested extending the notion of public space to encompass new spaces such as 'parking lots, shopping malls, vacation centres and cinema complexes.' He called these collective spaces and argued that architects should seek broader responsibility for their design. They should not concede their design to commercial logic and developer standards, but rather seek to transform them into challenging new fields of architectural investigation. De Solà-Morales described this task as 'the urbanisation of the collective territory.' The author continues:

"...the civic, architectural, urban and morphological richness of a contemporary city resides in the collective spaces that are not strictly public or private, but both simultaneously. These are public spaces that are used for private activities, or private spaces that allow for collective use, and they include the whole spectrum in between. Moreover, in the past decades the design of these collective spaces seems to have become an important modus operandi to intervene in the contemporary city. At the intersection between an architectural and an urban scale, architects and urban planners design projects that, through their character and hybridisation of privacy and publicity, contribute to the civic, typological and morphological richness of the city".[16]

The author suggests interconnecting private, enclosed spaces, to upgrade and turn them into parts of the collective realm: to include the particular in the sphere of the influence of the public. In order to do this, formal as well as informal processes of making collective spaces need to be monitored.

Proximity

The concept of depth and its corresponding models of proximity and accessibility are undoubtedly related to the use of space in a more exposed or intimate way, in a more collectively or individually used way. As mentioned before, depth was originally defined as the amount of boundary crossings needed to move from the outer space to the innermost territory. Outer space can often be related to public realm while the innermost territory often refers to private use of space. However, we might need to study these theoretical connotations: the configurational understanding of depth as a complex system of relations requires a profound study on what is understood as public and private and what are the relations in between. This refers to models of proximity. Proximity depends on individual or collective spacing mechanisms that define a certain model of space production and space organisation. Territorial depth as an access configuration can possess different recipes of proximity: each configuration is defined by a set of distances at different scales.

In 'Territory without a model' de Solà-Morales describes a different meaning of places, unlike the traditional genius loci concept: 'the expected sensation of voids and the indifference of its constructions'[17]. He refers to the rising importance of periphery that is no more based on tactics of repetition and differences but on a system of relative distances. As the dialogue between the building and the urban surrounding system became an individual one, distances lose their absolute value. They seem to belong to a more complex

1. de Solà-Morales, M. (1992). Public and Collective Space: The Urbanisation of the Private Domain as a New Challenge. In Oase, nº 33, reprinted in "A Matter of Things", Nai Publishers, Rotterdam 2008

2. Avermaete, T.; Hooimeijer F., Schrijver, L. (eds) (2007). Urban Formation and Collective Spaces. Rotterdam: OASE Journal for Architecture, Volume 71, NAi Publishers.

3. Scheerlinck, K. (2011). Privacy and Depth Configurations. Architektura & Urbanizmus. Journal for Architecture & Town Planning Theory, 2, 166-185.

4. Habraken, N.J. (1998). The Structure of the Ordinary. Cambridge: MIT Press.

5. Sennett, R. (2013). The Public Realm. Borders and Boundaries. Essay online: http://www.richardsennett.com.

6. Bijlsma, L., Groenland, J. (2008). The Intermediate Size: A Handbook for Collective Dwellings. Nijmegen: SUN.

7. Teerds, H.; Havik, K., Patteeuw, V. (2011). Productive Uncertainty, Indeterminacy in Spatial Design, Planning and Management. Oase #85. Rotterdam: NAi010 uitgevers.

8. ibid 4

9. ibid 4 p. 137

10. Hillier, B.; Hanson, J. (1984). The Social Logic of Space. Cambridge: University Press.

urban matrix. The author argues that the distance between areas or autonomous packages defines the very law that constructs peripheries; the notion of distance obtained an abstract dimension. However, the importance of this concept gets even more obvious by looking at it at the scale of the urban project; our daily experiences are now defined by sets of minimal or maximum distances. The distance between properties became important, as did the distances between properties and natural resources, between properties and infrastructures, and between properties and high employment areas. Instead of defining density, we ended up defining sets of rules of relative distances. These might be different in suburban conditions to downtown areas. In a way, we define and measure time and distance, comparing systematically with other configurations.

Spatial Delimitation

The next concept refers to spatial delimitation, an aspect that during the next decade will increasingly define the discourse on urban projects. It is becoming more important in response to issues of safety and security and at the same time to the different ways of upgrading social status and of differentiating yourself from your neighbor. The more you can afford to separate yourself from public life, the higher your social status becomes? Spatial mechanisms, and the increasing interest in spatially explicit boundary delimitations (fences and walls for example) relate to a new territorial balance mentioned by Ali Madanipour[18] and Richard Sennett.[19] On a global scale, and specifically in developing contexts, we can easily detect the increasing use of extreme fencing tactics and of spacing mechanisms with disproportionate physical distances. There seems to be a growing obsession about applying preplanned territorial transitions in urban projects, avoiding spontaneous overlap scenarios and restricting gaps or margins in the planning of depth configurations, as uncertainty in the interpretation of space is avoided.

Openness and functional indetermination

The last concept refers to openness, spatial tolerance and the needed discussion about the level of functional determination in urban projects. Lately, it seems as if projects or neighborhoods can no more be developed based on their spatial qualities and relations with the surrounding urban context but depend increasingly on programming spaces, as they often guarantee the financial backbone for development. Sebastien Marot[20] and Erik Van Daele[21] also mention this when reviewing contemporary urban or landscape projects. Over-programming and the exclusive focus on functional issues or even the description of ideal use or behaviour in urban space[22] lead to a simplification of urbanity and disable possible interpretations of multiple natures needed to construct a socially sustainable environment.

Conclusion

The reading and use of collective spaces, as an important part of inhabiting the urban landscape, is greatly changed due to environmental, economic and social developments. Changing climate, financial crisis and balancing employment rates, political regimes causing changes in ethnic or religious dominance and new flows of migration change the meaning of urban space and by that, its proper use and appropriation. Users change their behaviours, attitudes and claims to squares, gardens, streets and parks, responding to the incisive and profound changes of their daily reality and opportunities.

Collective space - today more than ever projected by academics, practitioners and stakeholders as multiple, flexible and open space - is contradictory to the apparent increasing need and desire to secure boundaries and claim spaces explicitly, in an individual as well as in a collective way. While the need to rethink and build new types of collective spaces grows,[23] more effort seems to be put into separating, delimiting and specialising urban space from the scale of the domicile to the scale of a neighborhood or the city. The Streetscape Territories research project seeks to study this balance of parallel mechanisms of space production in different contexts and to test the outcomes through real life projects, considering the local neighbourhood stakeholders as the main actors and beneficiaries.

11. Hillier, B. (1996). Space is the Machine. Cambridge: University Press.

12. ibid 11 p. 33

13. ibid 4

14. ibid 1 p. 3-8

15. Avermaete, T.; Teerds, H. (2007). Architectural Positions on the Public Sphere. The 2007 Delft Lecture Series, Places 19.2.

16. ibid 1 p. 3-8

17 de Solà-Morales, M. (1997). Territoris Sense Model. In Papers, Regió Metropolitana de Barcelona, nº 26. p. 21-27

18. Madanipour, A. (2003). Public and Private Spaces of the City. London: Routledge.

19. ibid 5

20. Marot, S.; Colafranceschi, D. (ed) (2006). Suburbanismo y el Arte de la Memoria. Madrid: Gustavo Gili.

21. Van Daele, E. (2014). Hybrids as Open Signifyers. Ghent/Brussels, doctoral thesis, Faculty of Architecture. Zukin, S. (1991). Landscapes of Power. Berkeley: University of California.

22. Sorkin, M. (2007). Indefensible Space: The Architecture of the National Insecurity State. New York: Routledge.

23. ibid 15

SHRINKING CITIES

BRENT D. RYAN

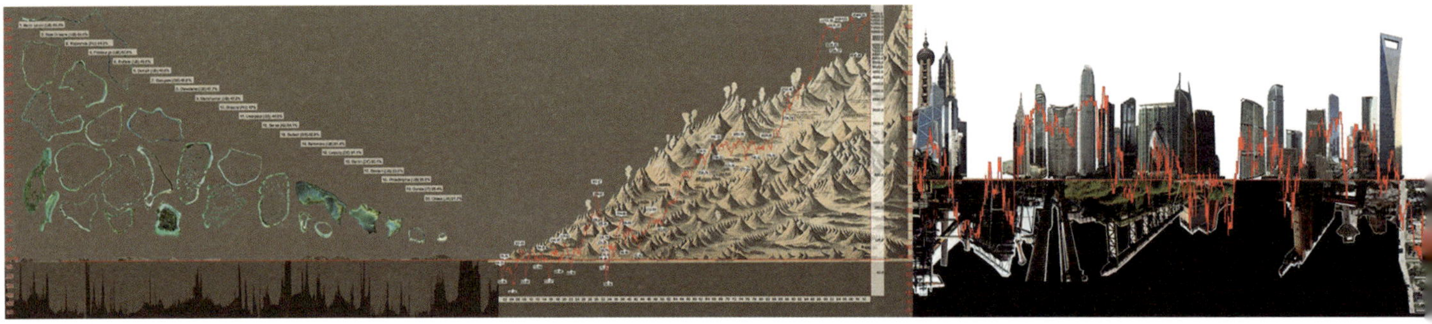

Shrinking cities, a term developed by German architect Philipp Oswalt around 2005, describes a heterogeneous group of cities that are mostly found in developed and de-industrialising nations. These cities are broadly characterised by a combination of population loss and building loss. Sometimes these losses are tremendous – up to 60 or 70 per cent population loss and 30 or 40 per cent of building loss.

The shrinking cities that are most visible to the design community are those where there has been either very rapid abandonment, as occurred in eastern Germany after 1990, or those cities where abandonment has gone on and on for decades without reversal, as in Detroit and many other American cities and other cities around the world.

Detroit is a highly visible, even iconic shrinking city, but in many ways it is unusual. Detroit was a very large city, one of the five largest in the United States in 1950. It underwent a radical deindustrialisation, losing about 90 per cent of its large automobile factories during the same period. It also underwent radical social change, shifting from a city that was about 80 per cent white in 1950 to one that was only ten per cent white in 2010.

Detroit's built environment is of great interest to designers because it is singular and in many ways difficult to comprehend as the city's urban fabric does not comply with normative urban visions. Detroit is a landscape of ruins, both of massive buildings like the former Packard Plant, and of thousands of abandoned houses. It is also a landscape of voids; the spaces left by former industry, commerce, infrastructure, and housing. I say landscape because in many ways Detroit is most easily understood as a giant post-industrial landscape.

The Causes

The causes of this decline are varied. Many cities are losing population because of demographic forces: people are aging, not having many children, not getting married, etc. However the largest force driving population and building loss is de-industrialisation. The former Soviet Union provides a good example of this. I visited Kherson, a city in Ukraine, where in the early 1990s the largest factories all shut down within a couple of years, because the Soviet economy collapsed and fragmented. Cotton processing and shipbuilding simply weren't needed any more, and the factories were old and obsolete. They were immediately abandoned and the sites have remained abandoned for the past twenty-five years, yet most of the buildings are still there.

We live in an era, as Manuel Castells said, where space is now a "space of flows". This is an elaborate way of saying that trade is increasing, capital transfers are increasing, and the principle of comparative advantage is growing ever stronger. Many former industrial cities simply cannot compete on the global market like they once did, especially in the new space of flows.

Role of the Discipline

An interesting study of New Haven, Connecticut was carried out by political scientist Douglas Rae. He attempted to actually quantify the amount of decline that was caused by the 'planning discipline' (really the urban renewal political apparatus, which included politicians, contractors, architects, etc.). Rae concluded that urban renewal, or intentional clearance and redevelopment of the urban fabric, had not caused the decline of New Haven 'in any simple way'. He concluded that technological advances, economic change and social preferences had caused decline much more than intentional replanning or redesign of cities.

I agree. When I looked at Detroit and Philadelphia in my book Design After Decline, I found that areas of the city that had not been rebuilt were often much worse off than areas that had been rebuilt. Lafayette Park is a good example. The rebuilt area has not declined, but the area around it has. Rem Koolhaas, looking at IIT, called this 'a metaphorical void in an actual void' – the void of Mies has become surrounded by a void of decline. So I think people who want to 'blame the planners' for the problems of cities like Detroit are pretty far off base.

Another irony is that the power of planners and urban designers to rebuild cities in the 1960s was much greater than the power that they have today, at least in the United States. This is not the case in Germany, where projects like the Emscher Landschaft-Park,

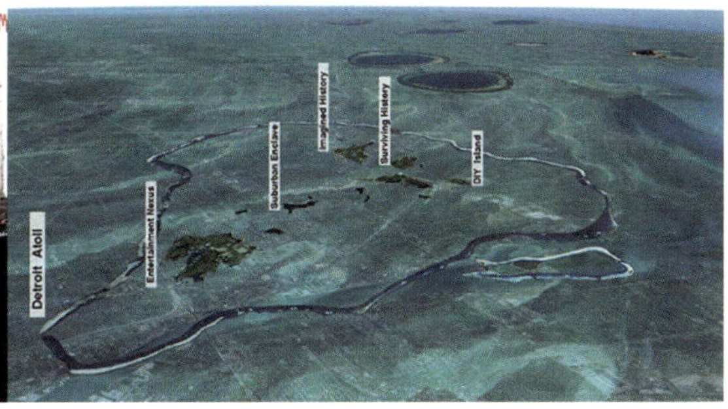

Left:
Atolls and Peaks: Topographical Landscapes of Poverty and Wealth

Middle:
The Fiscal Topography of Investment and Disinvestment

Right:
Detroit's Typological Archipelago

Image credits:
Lorena Bella Gomez

which is mostly from the 1990s and early 2000s, demonstrate that well-funded and intelligent design strategies, which include landscape, planning and architecture, can work wonders. Planners and designers looking to confront the problems of shrinking cities in the US today are mostly confined to low-cost or small-scale strategies. The reason for this is very simple: there is very little money to help shrinking cities.

So improvements are incremental, or bottom-up, or else they are conventional solutions that rely on public private partnerships – what Lynne Sagalyn called 'Downtown, Inc.' – to help shrinking cities. In Detroit these partnerships have constructed laudable projects like the Detroit Riverfront Park and Dequindre Cut bicycle path, and the Campus Martius Park. But partnerships are also constructing terrible projects like the new Detroit Red Wings stadium, which demolished an historic hotel just to build another parking garage. The role of government 'improvement' in Detroit is mixed.

Landscape, Infrastructural and the Human Condition

I always remind people that cities are made and inhabited by people, and that if designers forget the fact that people are going to inhabit their urban projects, then they are forgetting the key to their profession.

Certainly we must keep the same human condition in mind in shrinking cities. At the same time, to see shrinking cities as simply a human services problem is to ignore the benefits that creative urbanism can bring to a place. Why is an urban designer any less socially oriented than a social worker or public school teacher? I have always thought that shrinking cities provide an opportunity – and a motive – for urban designers to reconnect design and society.

It is interesting following on from this to look at the local solutions that are currently underway in shrinking cities around the world. In Germany, for example, the IBA is carried out in partnership with local actors – artists, citizens, designers, planners – but the IBA itself is a national idea. In the United States, almost every urban solution is a local solution, since there is no national design or planning policy. So Detroit is left on its own to generate solutions, although it can also engage national actors in generating those solutions.

Detroit's master plan FUTURE CITY, completed in 2012, was a local effort, paid for by a local foundation and engaging national and even international consultants including Toni Griffin and Stoss. Similarly, all of the Detroit park projects I mentioned earlier were local efforts, paid for by a consortium of local nonprofit groups and donors. Solutions can be local in another way – they can be site-based or episodic instead of systematic and widespread. Local scaled solutions tend to work well in shrinking cities, since the landscape is what I have called a 'patchwork' – it's divided into many different parts that are variably inhabited and uninhabited, with existing buildings or clusters of buildings surrounded by empty space.

This quality of Detroit's landscape led to what I called the 'fiscal archipelago' of the shrinking city in an article that my partner Lorena Bello and I wrote a couple of years ago. Essentially Detroit, though it is flat, can be seen as a series of islands – islands of architectural or urban interventions, even landscape interventions, which happen in places where profit is possible. We must remember that most of Detroit is very low value, and that construction in low value areas is very limited. Thus Detroit is like an atoll, with different built projects popping above the 'profit surface'.

With these local solutions regenerating space and challenging the way our cities function, I feel that shrinking cities offer designers the opportunity to completely reimagine the norms and means of urban design. Shrinking cities reconnects designers with the "social project" of Modernism that seemed to have evaporated. They provoke new ideals of what city form can be; they even made me reimagine the focus and purpose of urban design.

One of the big challenges (and opportunity) of our era is de-industrialisation – what to do with the places left behind by the decline of the industrial economy. The lessons and design ideas that we generate now will help designers in future decades deal with the decline of industry, and some ways that next generation of decline, and the next wave of solutions is already beginning to happen.

(Project)

ELECTROGEOGRAPHY: DESATURATED TERRITORIES

Courtney Goode, Nuith Morales & Yujin Yin

"As designers...we think of the electromagnetic spectrum as an inhabitable landscape, with its own electroclimate and electrogeography. But, like other 'natural' environments, the electromagnetic spectrum is constantly under threat from commercial over-development. Unsurprisingly, industry views hertzian space solely as something to be bought and sold...Unauthorized use is viewed as trespassing."[1]

Radio waves in the electromagnetic (EM) field are physical entities, although our senses are largely oblivious to them. They ripple around and through us, heavy with information, and folded into their volumes are political boundaries and economies. Urbanisation today is closely linked, even dependent on, the ability of EM waves to saturate the urban landscape with data. They function as dual commodity and territory.

As urbanisation increases, the EM field becomes a territorialised landscape in which frequencies are divided, auctioned and sold. Talk of a 'spectrum-shortage crisis'[2] generates pressure on the privatisation of the resource.

Electrogeography reinterprets conventional tools in landscape architecture –such as grading and planting design – by revealing their capacity to manipulate the region of the EM spectrum used by telecom companies and government entities. Surging landforms, reflective water bodies, and dense vegetation are known to interfere with, or entirely cut off, a range of EM signals[3]. Selectively clearing parcels of radio waves disrupts the path of urbanisation in the air and on the ground – establishing an operative framework that could be used to secure land for conservation (by decreasing its development value) or to foster the resurgence of shared experience in public space by cutting the personal tech-tether.

Joint Base Cape Cod (JBCC), a 22,000-acre military base currently occupying 10% of the Cape Cod peninsula, is the testing ground for the Electrogeography project. JBCC is undergoing transformative shifts in land use planning,[4] and is cradled by a ridge that naturally blocks high frequency radio waves, which cannot penetrate through terrain due to diffraction.[5]

Ridges and valleys are the primary components of the framework; the Ridge becomes the EM barrier, and the Valley the protected zone. The design prototype raises the height of the JBCC ridge, thereby increasing its range of influence. Dense vegetation is planted along its border to cause further diffraction,[6] and simultaneously provide a tactile experience. The design moves are basic, but they render a once invisible, highly trafficked territory legible on the ground.

Electrogeography is design through subtraction: removing EM traffic would shift portions of JBCC away from its current military program to become a testing ground for new forms of landscape and non-urbanized development. Electrogeography de-territorialises regions of the EM field to recondition a physical space; as the air is rid of intangible waves, all other senses saturate.

1. Dunne, A., Raby, F. (2001). Design Noir: The Secret Life of Electronic Objects. London: Basel, Switz.: August Media ; Birkhäuser.

2. Chen, Brian X. (2012). Carriers Warn of Crisis in Mobile Spectrum. The New York Times. Retrieved from http://www.nytimes.com/2012/04/18/technology/mobile-carriers-warn-of-spectrum-crisis-others-see-hyperbole.html?_r=1.

3. Collin, R. E. (1994). Full wave theories for rough surface scattering: An updated assessment, Radio Science.,29(5), 1237–1254, retrieved from doi:10.1029/94RS00745. http://onlinelibrary.wiley.com/doi/10.1029/94RS00745/full

4. The History of Planning at Joint Base Cape Cod. History of Planning at the JBCC. Retrived from http://www.thenationsfirst.org/JBCC/h-planning.html

5. ibid 3

6. Savage, N., D. Ndzi, A. Seville, E. Vilar, and J. Austin (2003), Radio wave propagation through vegetation: Factors influencing signal attenuation, Radio Science., 38, 1088, retrieved from doi:10.1029/2002RS002758, 5. http://onlinelibrary.wiley.com/doi/10.1029/2002RS002758/full

Opposite:
Clearing of signals from 100m above ground to touching the valley floor.

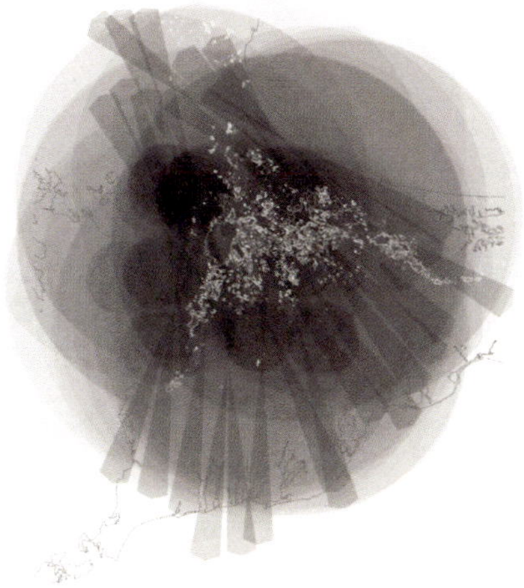

Left:
Map of potential signal shadow (white) caused by the ridge around Joint Base Cape Cod on nearby signals (grey).

Middle:
Map of towers transmitting EM signals in and around Joint Base Cape Cod.

Right:
Example of radio shadows on a single monotone signal volume.

Below:
Shadow Zones and Shaping Terrain:
Ridges attenuate all high frequency line-of-sight signals, creating a void; a shadow zone of desaturated air.

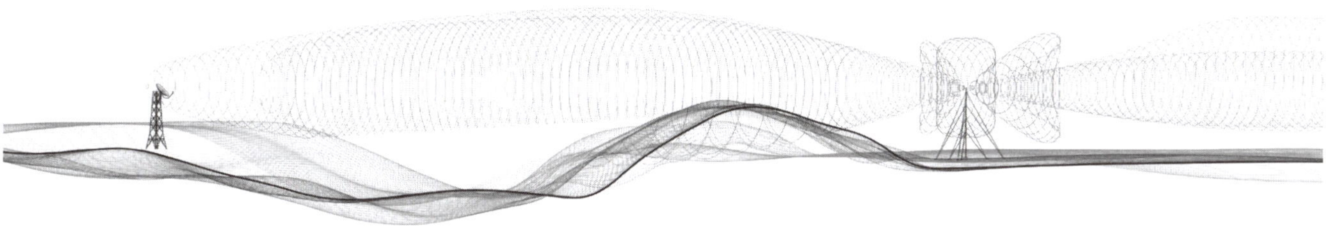

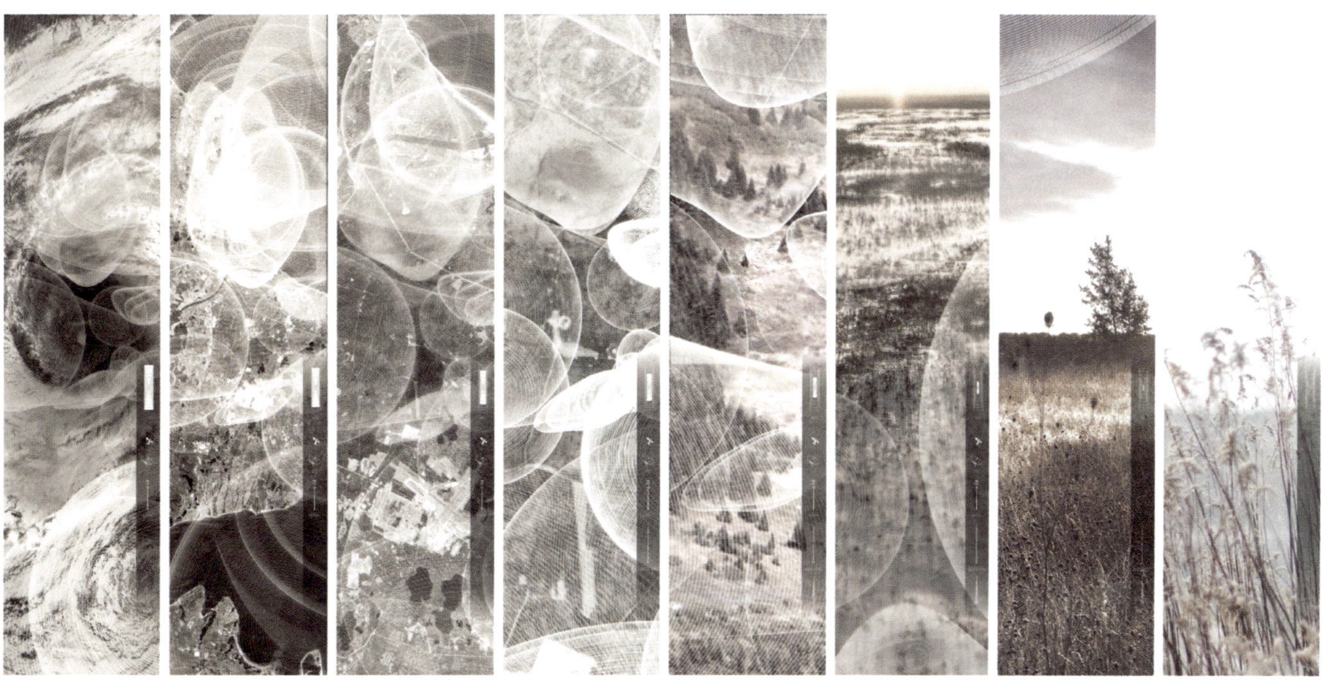

Jose Alfredo Ramirez Galindo & Clara Oloriz Sanjuan

:

BEYOND LAND: TOWARDS A TERRITORIAL PRAXIS

Within contemporary conditions, the impact of the discipline and profession of architecture is in some cases almost irrelevant to the production of our present world. Compared to other professions, economists, politicians, developers, policy-makers or computer scientists, architecture plays a tiny role in shaping our world, socially, politically and physically. Architecture seems to increasingly matter only to architects and the work that is produced admired for the singularity of the designed object; praised for its technical ability or aesthetic features but outside the realm of the majority's everyday life.

As an alternative, we argue for the emergence of 'territory' as a field of design praxis. Through the lens of territory, we can operate within contemporary conditions whereby urban environments are understood not as discrete independent collections of objects but rather as interconnected and related landscapes with specific and far reaching implications at local and global scales.

In this context 'territory' is seen as a framework from which to challenge normative practices in architecture and to reconceptualise the frameworks within which urban and landscape disciplines are conceived professionally today. The case of architecture is very symptomatic of this normative approach. It is being pushed aside as a mere service provider for the few, to the embellishment of punctual interventions in our cities or to provide efficient and economic schemes to deliver big profit for developers. Architecture is becoming more and more the means to materialise a given land value, to fulfil a maximum floor area ratio, complying with land use regulations, from a one-dimensional economic point of view.

In the case of urban disciplines, there exists a need to re-think new methods and categories through which we understand contemporary processes of urbanisation. As argued by Brenner,[1] current frameworks such as the so-called 'urban age' are responding not to contemporary processes and dynamics but rather to old modes that still see the city as a model for a 'universally generalisable settlement type'.[2] Today's urban reality 'has become more differentiated, polymorphic, variegated and multiscalar than in previous cycles of capitalist urbanisation'.[3] Requiring a re-conceptualisation of these frameworks from which to assess contemporary conditions, engage the urban reality, and intervene and project within it more effectively.

Normative approaches and old models of urban understanding have helped to reduce the role of design practices and we argue that this condition is intimately linked to the relationship between architecture and land, or rather the agency of architects and the way we understand the place on which architecture is grounded or even, the ground it constructs. In order to explain how this primordial relation, architecture-land, can be re-framed into what we call territorial praxis, we will depart from current uses and understanding of land and the potentials and opportunities 'territory' offers for its conceptual expansion.

1. Brenner, N, and Schmid, C. (2015). *Towards a new epistemology of the urban. City: analysis of urban trends, culture, policy, action*, 19, 2-3, pp. 151-182

2. Ibid. pp 151-158

3. Ibid 1. p 152

4. Elden, S. (2010). *Land, Terrain, Territory, Progress in Human Geography*, 34: 799 , pp. 804-811

5. Ibid. p 807

6. Ibid 4. p 809

7. Ibid 4. p 811

8. In a strict material sense, land is not generated, it is rather shifted. If we take into account the illegal sand mining that has provoked the disappearance of entire islands or the areas from Australia where sand was extracted to build Dubai's palm islands there is a shift in land, because sediment is a material that is shifted. For further reference see Sand Wars documentary

9. P.V. Aureli and M.Giudici, 'Architectural Association, Diploma 14: The Nomos of the Earth Brief' p. 7. https://www.aaschool.ac.uk/downloads/briefs2015/Diploma%2014_The%20Nomos%20of%20the%20Earth.pdf

10. Ibid

Satellite image showing Lake Manzala, in the Northeast part of the Nile Delta, and its radical land transformation though erosion and siltation, within a span of 40 years.

Elden's Territory

The term land, seen as a finite commodity that can be distributed, bought and sold, is according to Elden 'a relation of property' becoming a 'political-economic question.'[4] Considering the space on which architecture sits as land related to property, in a reductionist way, produces a mentality in which architecture is left to materialise the potential profit existing in land value. This can be explained as a consequence of taking the limited notion of land for territory or reducing territory to land as Elden's reading of Lefebvre highlights.[5] So, here instead of using the term land, we will refer to this idea of territory, to emphasise the fact that it includes land and terrain 'but it is more than this.' It is also dependent on a number of techniques, like geography, cartography or land surveying to measure the land and the law for controlling the terrain or ´political technologies´[6] 'in terms of its mapping, ordering, measuring and demarcation and the way it is normalised, circulation allowed, and internally regulated,' according to Elden. 'Land' and 'Terrain' represent respectively the 'political-economic' and the 'political-strategic' questions of territory which are essential but at the same time insufficient to understand territory, in Western terms.[7]

Territory is 'a word, a concept and a practice' in which various 'calculative strategies' such as cartography are complicit agencies in its design. Acknowledging this, we argue about the possibility of engaging with a territorial praxis through two particular examples from the Architectural Association Landscape Urbanism Programme and Elden's conceptual framework. Architecture and the ability to design, organise, coordinate and choreograph spaces can and should go beyond the reductive relation between architecture and land. We assert that in order to do this, we need to rethink the framework of our interventions in order to claim a different agency and engage in a relevant conversation with other professions.

The Construction of Territory

We are going to explore this definition of a territorial project, implicit in architecture's relationship with land, through two projects in which on the one hand land, even though being a finite source,[8] can be generated by means of reclamation projects or disappeared through erosion forces (see Lake Manzala satellite images) and on the other hand, land can be redistributed, subdivided or combined, as a response to government's irrigation management (see Project Two: Flooding Mechanisms). Seen from the perspective of a quantifiable commodity, land re-distribution and generation pose several questions in relationship to its strategic normalization and its dependence on the law, measure and calculation. Both operations, land reclamation and redistribution are enabled through infrastructural projects in which land is dredged and redistributed through engineering water policies. They reveal the agency of the supposedly scientific infrastructure as a medium for the facilitation, construction or mutation as indexes of the political forces at stake.

11. Ibid 9. p 9

12. 'Infrastructures [...] operate 'Between Nature, Culture, Society, Technology and Politics'. As such, they play a fundamental, and increasingly significant, role as the apparatus through which the material, social and economic flows which constitute the territory of globalised capitalism are captured, processed, organised and (unevenly) distributed.' E. Castro, A. Ramirez, E. Rico and D. Spencer. Critical Territories From Academia to Praxis (London, List, 2013), p. 9

13. L. Mourtiz, C. Tin-Fu, X. Hu. 'Littoral Negotiations', Architectural Association Landscape Urbanism (London, 2014-15), p. 47. https://issuu.com/aalandscapeurbanism/docs/littoral_negotiations

14. Ibid 4. p 810

15. Ibid 4. p 812

16. Ibid 13

17. Ibid 13. p 13

18. Ibid

19. S. Ribot Gil, L. Driva, D. Bra, 'Flooding Mechanisms', *Architectural Association Landscape Urbanism* (London, 2014-15), p. 18-25. https://issuu.com/aalandscapeurbanism/docs/flooding_mechanisms_aa_landscape_ur.

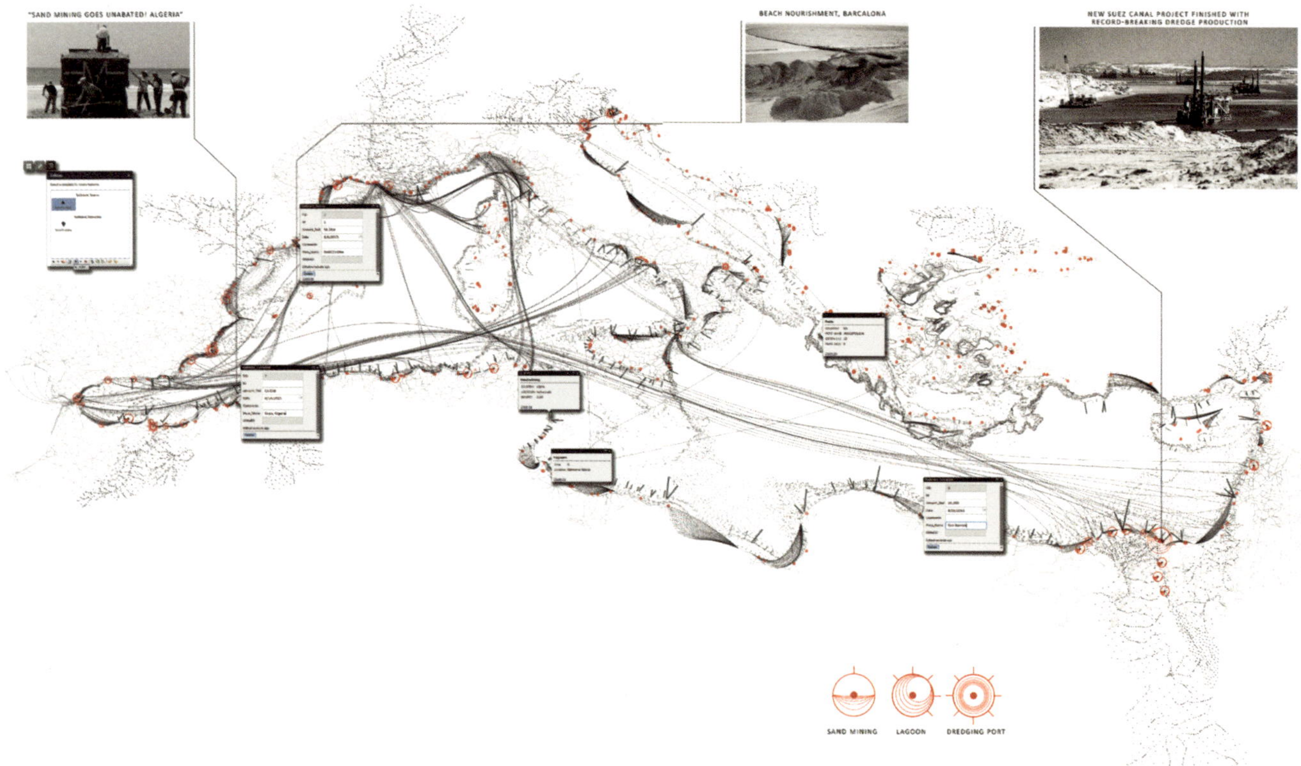

Littoral Negotiations: Cartographic Atlas of the Mediterranean Sea unveiling the existing sediment movement across the region.

In this sense, we refer here to Aureli's notion of 'the architecture of the territory' in which 'limits, boundaries, thresholds, topography, topology, logistics, and infrastructure become direct indexes of the way political forces directly inform human subjectivity.'[9]
It is interesting to note here that Aureli argues that 'the accumulation of capital' in cities from the 12th century and the consequent territorial hierarchy unbalances the Roman tension between nomos - the act of defining and parceling a territory in order to give a form to it- and the urbs -movement, circulation and territorial power expansion of the city. Aureli adds that 'starting from the medieval city, economy becomes increasingly more powerful than politics and the latter is made into an ideological lubricant for the success of the former.'[10] Thus, we can see here that the economic wealth or the strategic-economic aspect of territory defined by Elden takes prevalence in its definition, concealing the political technology and political strategy. According to Aureli, with the last form of nomos 'Territory loses its legibility' at the same time as architecture rises as a specific discipline: 'Since architecture is ennobled as an intellectual profession it focuses mainly on prestigious commissions such as churches, palaces and public buildings. All infrastructural works such as roads, walls, dams, land reclamation are left to the anonymous domain of engineering. The territory is thus constructed following a mere managerial logic that leaves no room for physical representation.'[11]

Along similar lines, Critical Territories. From Academia to Praxis' introduction summarises Graham's contribution 'Infrastructural Turn' as the apparatus that organises 'the material, social and economic flows which constitute the territory of globalised capitalism.'[12] Following Elden's affirmation about cartography being complicit in the production of territory and taking Graham's questioning of engineering, we can state that engineering infrastructures and architecture are 'political technologies' complicit in its construction. Thus, through the following two examples, we argue about the agency of the architect in the construction and even the design of the territory as a territorial praxis.

Project One: Littoral Negotiations

Littoral Negotiations, by Liam Mouritz, Chang Tin-Fu and Xiabin Hu proposes an alternative form of understanding land ownership and coastal rights in the invisible sediment transboundary distribution across the Mediterranean Sea. In the last century, sediment has been trapped in dam constructions, depriving the sea from river sediments and thus, increasing erosion.

20. 'Dams, inter-river basin transfers, large-scale irrigation coupled with massive hydroelectric development transformed the hydro-social cycle in radical ways, thereby producing new socio-ecological configurations in a hybridized landscape that fuses together things natural and social.' E. Swyngedouw, (2015) *Liquid Power. Contested Hydro-Modernities in Twentieth-Century Spain.* Cambridge, MA., The MIT Press), p. 4

21. 'Not a drop of water should reach the ocean without paying its obligatory tribute to the earth (Cortes Generales, Spanish parliament, 1912).' E. Swyngedouw, (2015) *Liquid Power. Contested Hydro-Modernities in Twentieth-Century Spain.* Cambridge, MA., The MIT Press. p. 4.

22. Ibid 20. p 14

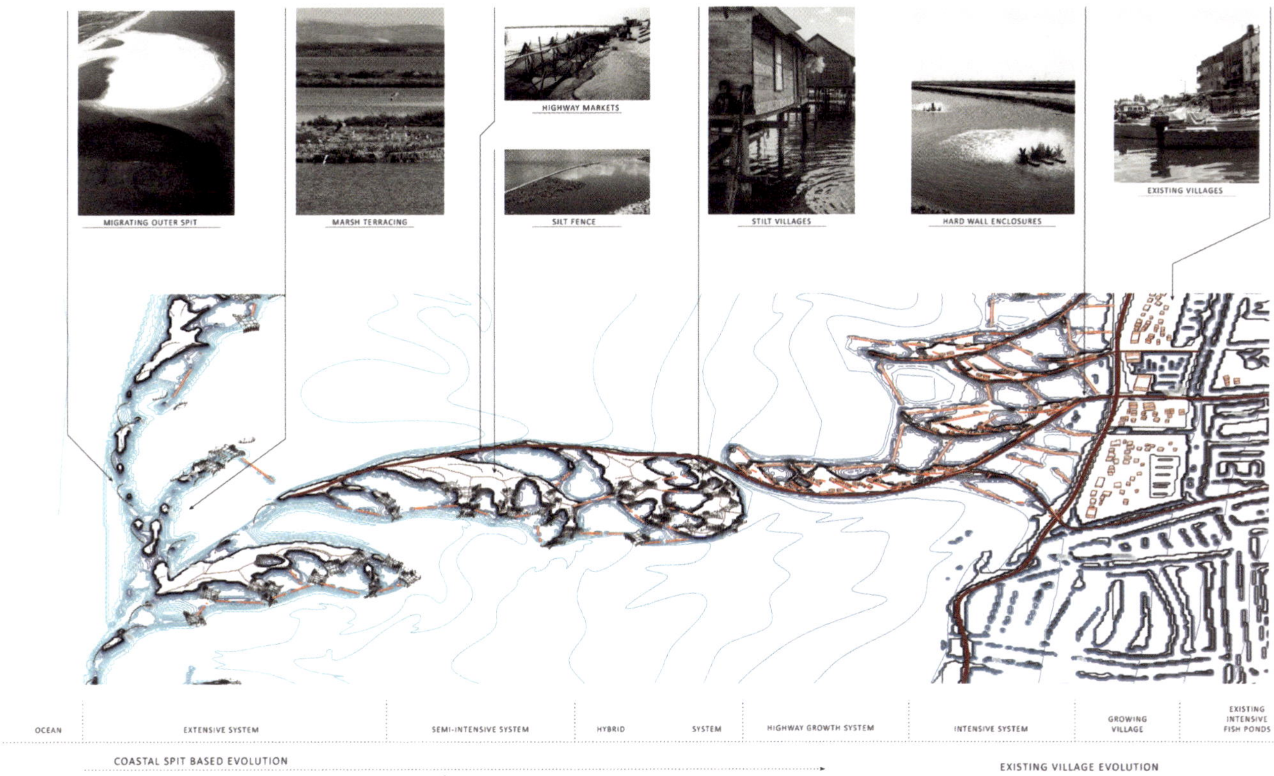

Littoral Negotiations:
Cartography of the sedimentation process design in accordance to its social and geomorphological conditions.

This project looks at the dredging projects in the Mediterranean Sea related to the expansion of the Suez Canal to accommodate larger ships. As a consequence, the Mediterranean ports are expected to grow and generate an artificial surplus of sediments in the sea. In particular, it looks at the Nile delta and how the lack of sediments due to dam engineering projects from the 1960's is provoking the erosion of its river mouth. This triggers the disappearance of owned land and increases the risk of coastal erosion in lake Manzala. In this area, the local economy is based on fish farm production at various scales: from small illegal structures to larger intensive production facilities that have proliferated in the last four decades due to Egypt's growing population and protein demands, filling and silting the lake.[13] Thus, within these local and global economies, engineering consequences and sediment dynamics, these students propose the use of local fish farming techniques -net and sticks- to catch sediment in order to protect lake Manzala but also to expand its production into the sea.

The sediment management strategy is based on the distribution of sediments coming from the Suez Canal in the tip of the Nile delta, using use the sea currents. The organisation of a series of fish ponds catches sediment, gradually consolidating land and infrastructure for the fish farms. Various deployment scenarios through time where the aggregation of these fish pens becomes a larger structure trigger temporary forms of association between the individual farmers. In this proposal, the land is not owned permanently and public infrastructure is constructed through cooperatives. This form of land generation requires time, collective production at multiple scales and it is subject to the variations in sediment supply, which can both generate but also dissolve land. The criteria to design the sedimentation process is based on the existing production types and agencies, from the small illegal fish pens to the larger intensive farms, and the geomorphological conditions.

An alternative understanding of land, that is not finite or permanent, or that cannot be owned, demands a redefinition of the social and spatial modes of organization and management, as well as innovative techniques to measure it and control its terrain, in Elden's terms: how this 'concept of 'space' as a political category' can be 'owned, distributed, mapped, calculated, bordered and controlled?'[14] These questions pose the challenge of a multidisciplinary approach to re-think political techniques or 'measure and control -the technical and the legal- [...] alongside land and terrain.'[15] Our scope as architects is limited to deal with legal

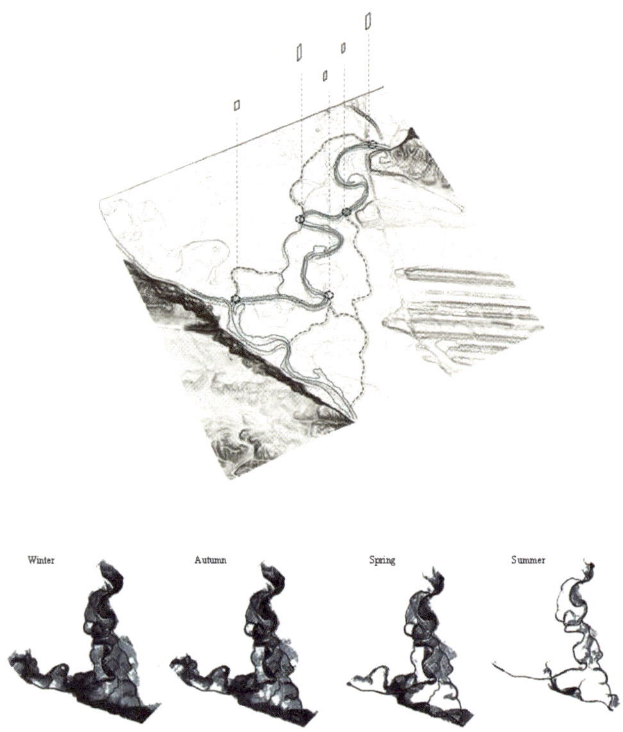

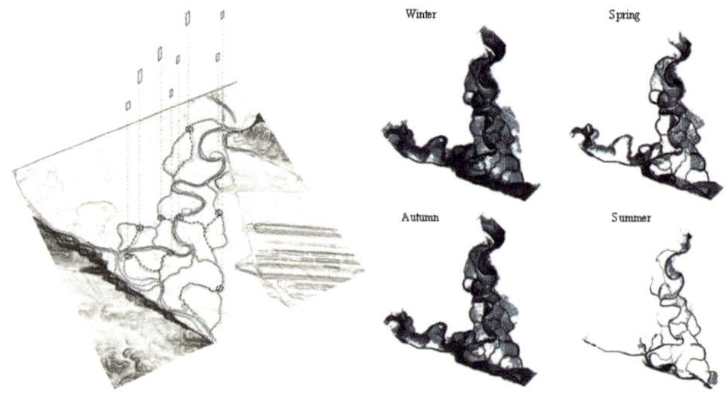

Triggering Avulsions, Stage 2.

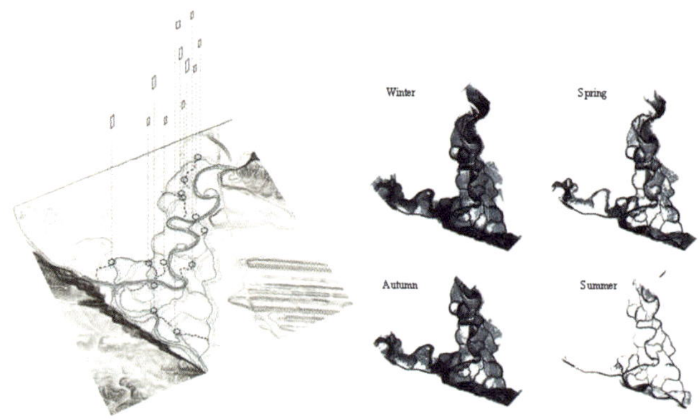

codes or other aspects of territorial projects, but an awareness about the consequences and compromises of our design decisions, or rather a more transdisciplinary or maybe even a non-disciplinary form of design, can challenge our contemporary position as service providers, which does not compartmentalise or isolate the manifold aspects of territory.

Here, students propose a framework for a territorial project, positioning themselves in the 'politics of sediment'[16] distribution, understanding that a land reclamation or dredging technique cannot be deployed disregarding its 'political economic' or 'political strategic' aspects. They also positioned themselves critically towards the global 'sand wars'[17] and land reclamation projects such as Dubai.[18] This project shows how 'the production of space,' and construction of territory has political, economic and also, material consequences with which we think architects have the potential to engage in transdisciplinary projects.

Project Two: Flooding Mechanisms

Flooding Mechanisms, by Silvia Ribot Gil, Lida Driva and Dimitra Bra, addresses European water policies that sit between efficient engineering irrigation systems to maximize agricultural production or 'resource' approach and the 'ecologic approach' of initiatives like 'room for the river' to deal with flooding issues.[19] More, in particular, this project critically explores the consequences of the construction of the second phase of a reservoir and canal system to irrigate agricultural areas along the rivers Ega and Arga in North Spain. The implementation of this canal system comes with a governmental regulation law –considered by Elden as a political technology- that sets the minimum area of an agricultural plot to be benefited from this system to five Ha. In twelve years the spatial organisation of small parcels fuses into larger plots. The consequences of this irrigation infrastructure, not only affect the political-strategic or the political-economic in terms of laws and land ownership, but trigger a form of agricultural production based on large-scale monoculture that provokes high peaks in water demands, but also in labour (for instance in the harvesting time when temporary and illegal workers come to this area) and market economy scales.

The canal extension project can only be understood within the framework of water policies in Spain in the 20th and 21st centuries as Erik Swyngedouw brilliantly puts it in 'Liquid Power: Contested Hydromodernities in Twentieth Century Spain'.[20]

Flooding Mechanisms:
Productive Actualisation Manual:
Strategic deployment of landscapes techniques such as small excavation and weirs to gradually provoke avulsions and erode the designed irrigation system.

23. 'Territory must be approached politically in its historical, geographical and conceptual specificity.' 'Territory as a distinctive mode of social/spatial organization, one which is historically and geographically limited and dependent, rather than a biological drive or social need.' S. Elden, (2010) *Land, Terrain, Territory, Progress in Human Geography*, 34: 799. p 810

24. Ibid 19

25. S. Elden, (2013). *The Birth of Territory.* Chicago and London, The University of Chicago Press. p 17

Seasonal Flooding

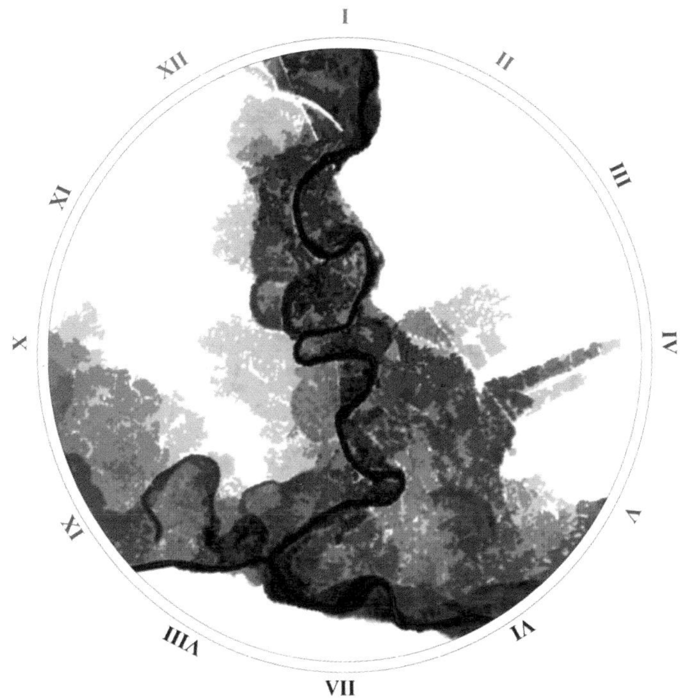

Flooding Scenario

Flooding Mechanisms: Geomorphology: Study Area Flooding: Cartography depicting the flooding seasonal cycles of the river Arga and Aragon. This cycle is neglected by the managerial approach imposed by the irrigation canal system approach.

As a result, 'today every single one of the ten mainland river basins (in Spain) is fully engineered, monitored and manicured [...] often to the last drop'[21] in great part due to Franco's dictatorship 'wet dream' which unfolded a 'techno-natural' revolution.[22] There are two main ideas we can extract from Swyngedouw's argument, on the one hand the fact that water policies and infrastructure cannot be taken in isolation from their political, social and economic consequences. On the other hand, as stressed by Elden, how historically and geographically dependant and limited, specific territorial organisations are, rather than biologically driven or by a social need.[23]

The use of river flooding mechanisms and small-scale engineering weirs produces an agricultural land for a small-scale production and of distinctive agricultural quality, negotiating with crops' water demand and flooding times. This alternative for water distribution produces a territory that reveals how the various irrigation techniques produce particular forms of spatial organisation, land ownership, and resource management. This project proposes new units of management as the tools for governance and control: 'Micro-flooding unit development.'[24]

Agency and Territorial Praxis

These interventions and their consequences in land re-distribution, reveal how the territory is a 'process, made and remade, shaped and shaping, active and reactive'[25] according to Elden. They show that architecture and infrastructural technologies construct and re-construct land, and therefore are part of the territorial process.

Territory is the place or the lenses through which architecture is produced and inversely, the latter is also part of the construction of territory. Architecture and infrastructure as technologies in the broadest sense are in a way complicit in the construction of territory, its materialisation. The profession's agency has relegated itself to the design of commissioned projects in the last stage of the territorial project, giving concrete form to a plot of land or planning regulation set by managerial guidelines where architects are not part of the conversation. It is key to regain relevance and to engage with today's pressing conditions to build a critical awareness about the role of architecture and the agency of the designer in the construction of the territorial project.

X P A

EXPANSION EXPANSION EXPA

EXPA

PA A

EXPANSION

ON SI

E XP PA

EXPANSION EXPANSION

EXPANSION

NS

X P A

SI

NS I

EXPA

SI

EXPANSION EXPAN ON

EXPAN ION EXPANS N EXPANSIO EXPA

EXPA

EXPAN ION EXPANS N EXPANSIO EXPA

EXPA

XP IO PA

EXPAN ION EXPANS N EXPANSIO EXP

EXP

EXPANSION

S I O

ION EXPANSION EXPANSION

ION

IO

EXPANSION

I IO N

EXPANSION EXPANSION

EXPANSION

S I O

PA

AN

ION

PA

EX ANSION EXPANSION

I

ION XPANSION E ANSION EXP NSION

I

ION

ION XPANSION E ANSION EXP NSION

I

ION

SI XP ION

ION XPANSION E ANSION EXP NSION

ION

EXPANSION

Christian Schmid,
Neil Brenner,
Milica Topalovic

:

CARTOGRAPHIES OF PLANETARY URBANISATION

Today, urbanisation has become planetary. The boundaries of the urban have been exploded to encompass vast territories far beyond the limits of even the largest megacity regions. Meanwhile, novel patterns of urbanisation are crystallising, which challenge inherited conceptions of the urban as a bounded, universal settlement type.

Cartographies of Planetary Urbanisation is an exhibition proposing a radical rethinking of inherited cartographies of the urban. The popular claim that we now live in an 'urban age' because the majority of the world's population live in 'cities', is a deeply misleading basis for understanding the contemporary 'urban revolution', theorised by Henri Lefebvre. Cities are not isolated manifestations or universally replicated expressions of the urban condition, but are embedded within wider, territorially uneven and restlessly evolving processes of urbanisation at all spatial scales. Encompassing both built and unbuilt spaces, across earth, water, sea and atmosphere.

In this exhibit, shown at the 2015 Shenzhen Biennale of Architecture/Urbanism: Radical Urbanism, interdisciplinary research teams from the ETH Zürich, ETH Future Cities Laboratory Singapore and the Urban Theory Lab at the Harvard Graduate School of Design, presented new frameworks for understanding and representing contemporary forms of urbanisation through three interrelated lines of inquiry:

1. Comparative analysis of the urbanisation processes that have transformed Tokyo, Hong Kong/Shenzhen/Dongguan, Kolkata, Istanbul, Lagos, Paris, Mexico City and Los Angeles. We explode the singular notion of the city to explore, in comparative perspective, differing patterns and pathways of urbanisation in some of the world's most dynamically changing urban territories.

2. The extension and thickening of the urban fabric in some of the planet's supposedly most 'remote' or 'wild' zones – the Amazon, the Arctic, the Gobi desert, the Himalayas, the Sahara, Siberia, the Pacific Ocean and the earth's atmosphere. Even these sparsely populated areas are today experiencing a massive intensification of land use, the construction of new connectivity infrastructures, and accelerated socio-environmental transformation to support the world's major population centres.

3. The transnational hinterland archipelago that supports urbanisation in Singapore, one of the world's most globally networked agglomerations. In contrast to standard representations of cities as self-propelled economic powerhouses, we track the wide-ranging flows of food, water, energy, sand and labor-power that support this growing, globally strategic urban centre. Instead of the city-state, we propose the cross-border metropolitan region as the new urban paradigm for Singapore.

The exhibition highlights the interplay between the search for new theoretical concepts, territorially grounded studies of specific patterns and pathways of urbanisation, and the use of cartography to decipher new geographies of urbanisation for which we currently lack an adequate analytical or representational vocabulary.

Arctic
The strategic/speculative space of the Arctic: oil fields, projected oil reserves, pipelines and shipping routes.
Map Credits:
Grga Basic & Urban Theory Lab

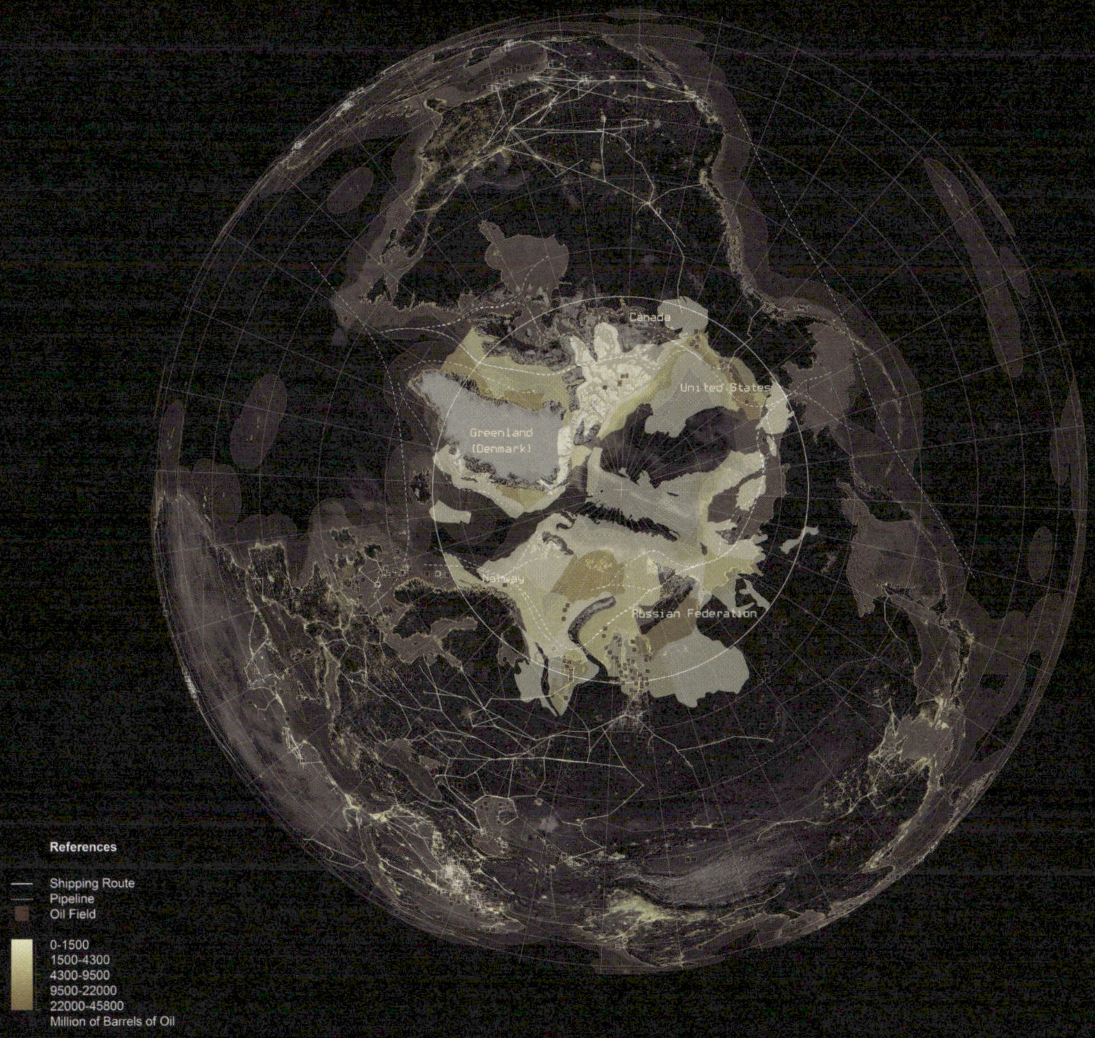
Canada
United States
Greenland
(Denmark)
Norway
Russian Federation
References
Shipping Route
Pipeline
Oil Field
0-1500
1500-4300
4300-9500
9500-22000
22000-45800
Million of Barrels of Oil

METROPOLITAN PROCESSES

CHRISTIAN SCHMID

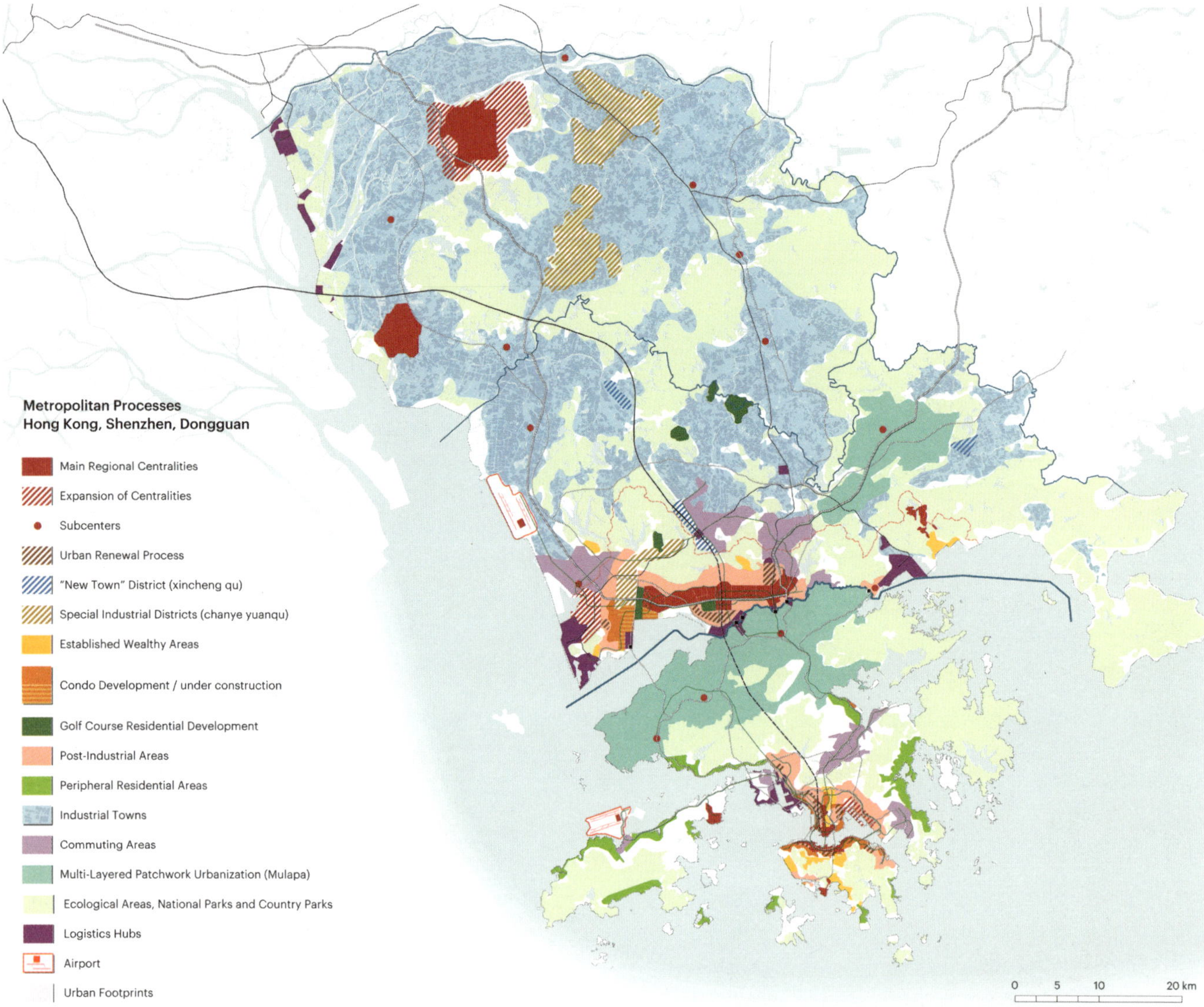

The last two decades have seen a sharp increase in the speed, scale and scope of urbanisation that has fundamentally changed the character of urban areas. Transcending physical borders, political jurisdictions and social spheres, urbanisation has become a planetary phenomenon. Urban forms associated with relatively stable human settlement spaces – often represented as dots on a rural background – are superseded by increasingly heterogeneous, complex and polymorphous urban regions. This diversification of urban forms has important implications for urban planning and design. It demands a comparative and synoptic approach that can both grasp the processes of planetary urbanisation and remain sensitive to the diversifying local manifestations. A new vocabulary of urbanisation is required to help us decipher the rapidly mutating landscapes of urbanisation that are today being produced across the planet.

By analysing and comparing eight large metropolitan areas, this research project elaborates the processes of urbanisation to explain how general tendencies are materialised in specific places. We analysed the urbanisation processes in the individual metropolitan regions on the ground, and brought them conceptually into conversation with each other. With a multidimensional methodological design that combines a wide variety of sources and procedures we generated a series of maps that show the main urban configurations for each city. In a next step we compared these maps and identified a range of urbanisation processes that are emerging in several of these

Metropolitan Processes:
Hong Kong, Shenzhen, Dongguan
The Eastern side of the Pearl River Delta can be characterised as a multi-scalar, polycentric and cross-border metropolitan area. This territory has emerged from the dialectics of fixity and motion that has triggered the leapfrogging urbanisation of South China.
Map Credits:
Tammy Kit Ping Wong &
Philippe Rekacewicz

Metropolitan Processes:
Los Angeles is famous for its polycentrism as well as for its never-ending sprawl. In this map we have brought a semblance of order to a city that many have considered immanently illegible.
Map Credits:
Ozan Karaman, Christian Schmid,
Rob Sullivan & Philippe Rekacewicz

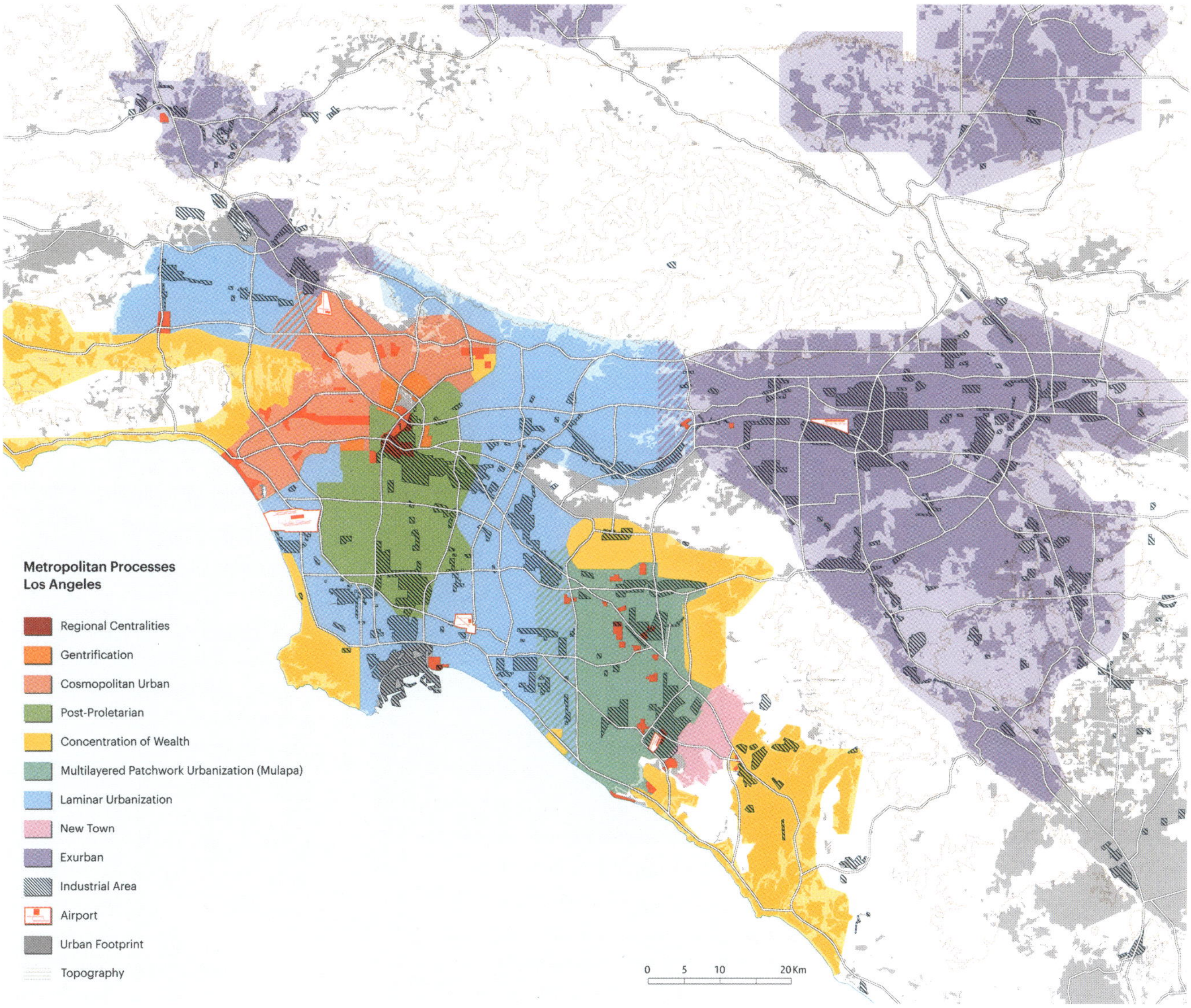

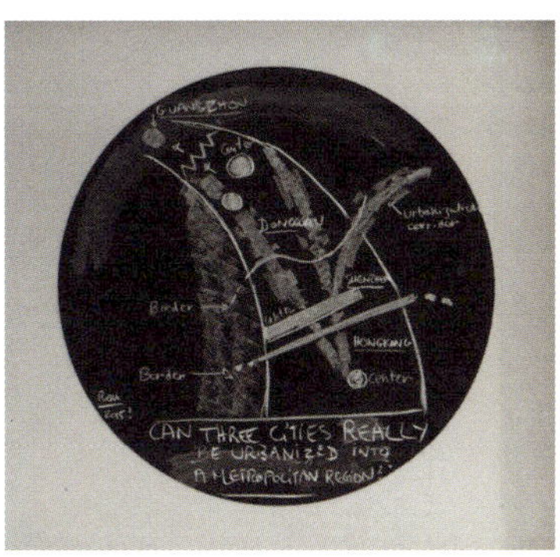

Cartographic Performance:
Philippe Rekacewicz, French cartographer, geographer and journalist, together with project participants and the audience, made a cartographic performance using the blackboard "maps:" and "globes" mounted on the facade of the exhibition rotunda.

Exhibition Photography:
Bas Princen

urban regions. The particular processes to be compared and the categories of comparison themselves were not pre-determined. This comparative procedure enabled us to group together specific processes that have a number of common features and dynamics, and to develop a set of comparative categories of contemporary urbanisation. It finally allows us to systematically analyse the diversity of responses to many of the common challenges posed by contemporary urbanisation, such as urban sprawl, the commodification of space, socio-spatial segregation, housing for the poor, renewal of old housing stock, and the development of urban differences in terms of their effectiveness, their unintended consequences, and their ramifications for the quality of everyday urban life.

OPERATIONAL LANDSCAPES

NEIL BRENNER

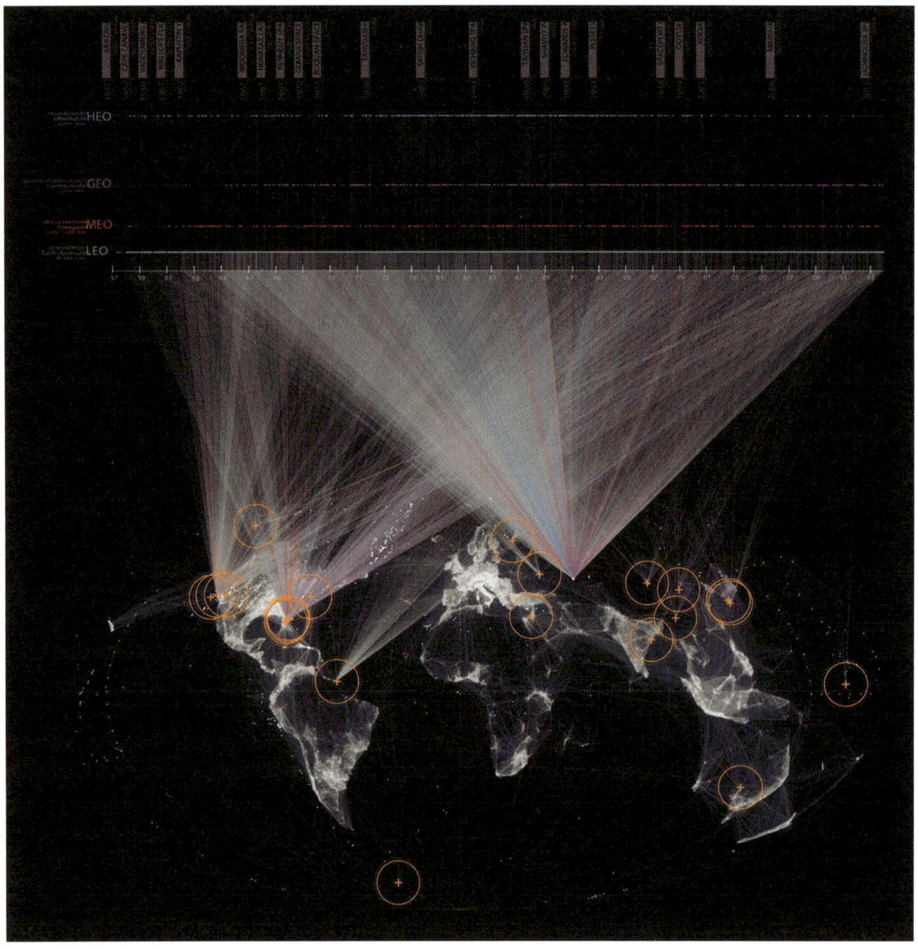

Atmosphere:
The earth's atmosphere has been transformed into a field of logistical coordination in support of urban life.
Map Credits:
Chris Bennett, Urban Theory Lab

Exhibition Photography:
Bas Princen

In what sense do we today live in an 'urban age'? This idea is frequently invoked by scholars, policy-makers, planners, designers and architects, usually with reference to the proposition that more than 50% of the world's population now lives within cities. But, can the nature of our urban world be understood and mapped exclusively with reference to the growth of cities and their populations?

Our current work with the Urban Theory Lab (urbantheorylab.net) turns this proposition upside-down and inside-out by speculating on a radically alternative mapping of contemporary planetary urbanisation. Rather than focusing our attention on large population centres, we investigate urbanisation from the point of view of its putative 'outsides', the zones that are commonly represented as rural, remote, wild and/ or untouched by human impact.

What happens to our cognitive map of the global urban condition if we focus not on the global cities or mega-cities of the world, but on the wide-ranging socio-spatial and environmental transformations that are currently unfolding in supposedly 'remote' or 'wilderness' regions, such as the Amazon, the Arctic, the Gobi desert steppe, the Himalayas, the Pacific ocean, the Sahara desert and Siberia, and even the earth's atmosphere? To what degree are such zones now being integrated within a worldwide fabric of urbanisation? How are they being restructured and enclosed to support the energy, water, material, food and logistics needs of major cities?

Through a combination of historical analysis, critical geopolitical and economic evaluation, as well as geospatial data visualisation and conceptual experimentation, this research aims to extend the analytical and political horizons of urban theory into these 'extreme territories' of urbanisation.

Amazon:
Today, the urban fabric of the Amazon is being dramatically thickened in support of planetary urbanisation.
Map Credits:
Ali Fard, Daniel Ibanez and others in the Urban Theory Lab

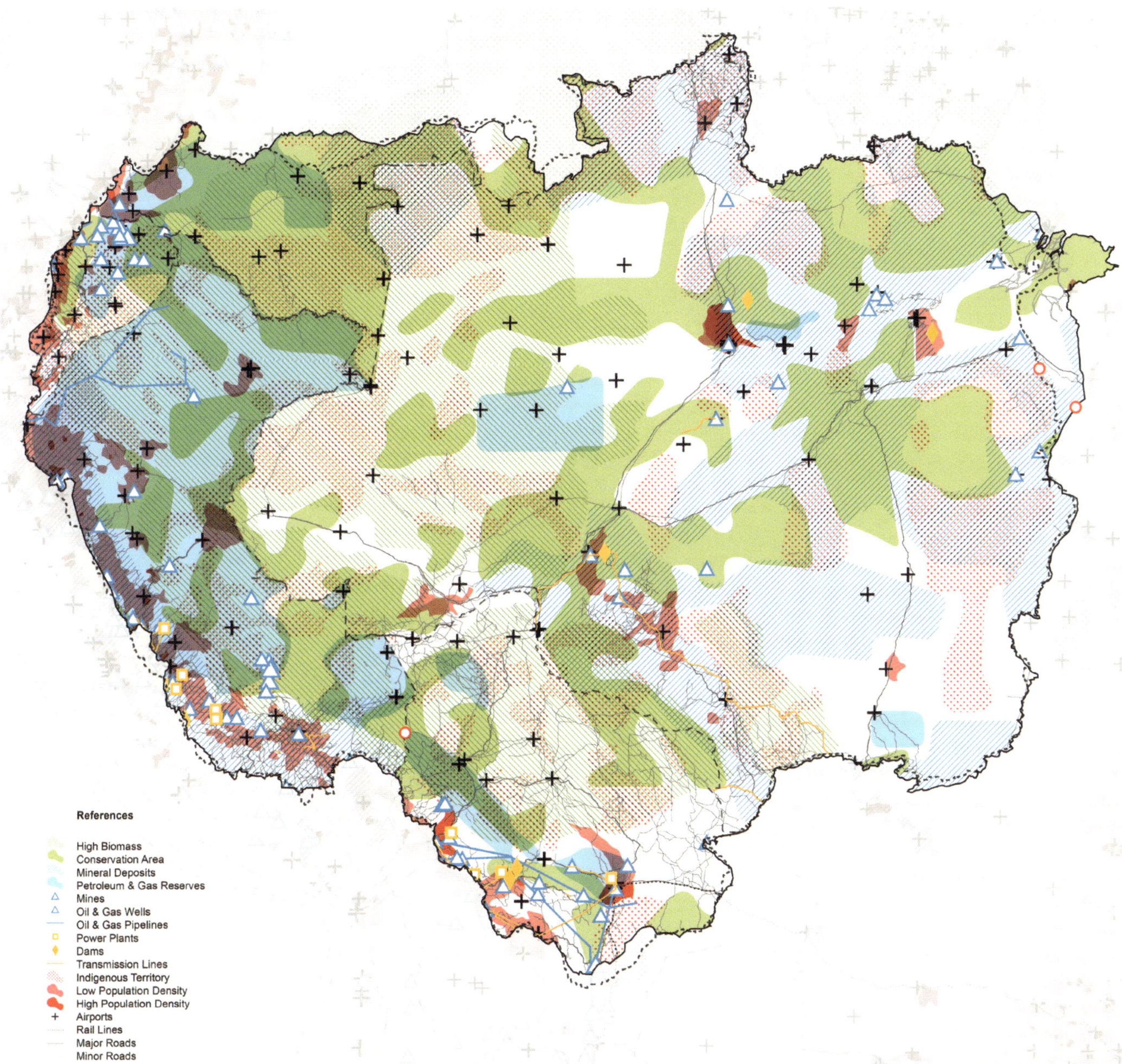
References
High Biomass
Conservation Area
Mineral Deposits
Petroleum & Gas Reserves
Mines
Oil & Gas Wells
Oil & Gas Pipelines
Power Plants
Dams
Transmission Lines
Indigenous Territory
Low Population Density
High Population Density
Airports
Rail Lines
Major Roads
Minor Roads

HINTERLAND: SINGAPORE BEYOND THE BORDER

MILICA TOPALOVIC

Throughout history, cities have functioned as centres of political and economic power, from which the agricultural and resource-rich hinterlands were controlled. From the nineteenth century onward, new technologies, transportation modes and the opening of trade have introduced a remarkable complexity to the relationship between cities and territories. Today, it is often thought that cities rely decreasingly on surrounding territories for supply and subsistence. Instead, they seem emancipated from the constraints of geography, operating in a global web of dependencies. By contrast, this research is based on a hypothesis that an understanding of the city-territory relationship, the ability to conceptualise it in qualitative terms, and to influence it by means of planning and design strategies, is central in addressing urban sustainability.

At first glance, the island city-state of Singapore is the 'city without a hinterland'. Certainly, it is a city whose production grounds and vital resources lie beyond national borders. The economic incorporation of hinterland territories in Malaysia, Indonesia, Southern Asia and beyond, have remained both a necessity and a profitable opportunity for Singapore.

The research concerns the problematic of Singapore's hinterland at various territorial scales, from local to global. The five key resources for Singapore – sand, water, food, oil and human labour – as well as territorial dynamics of resource extraction, flows and accumulation at

Singapore island republic and the urbanised sea of the Singapore Straight.
Credits:
Bas Princen:
Anchorage Zone
(Singapore Straight), 2015

Cross Border Metropolitan Region
Singapore, Johor, Riau Archipelago:
Territories of Urbanisation
The regional picture of Singapore shows that its productive hinterlands in Indonesia and Malaysia are experiencing fast population growth and urbanisation.
Map Credits:
Karoline Kostka

Exhibition Photography:
Bas Princen

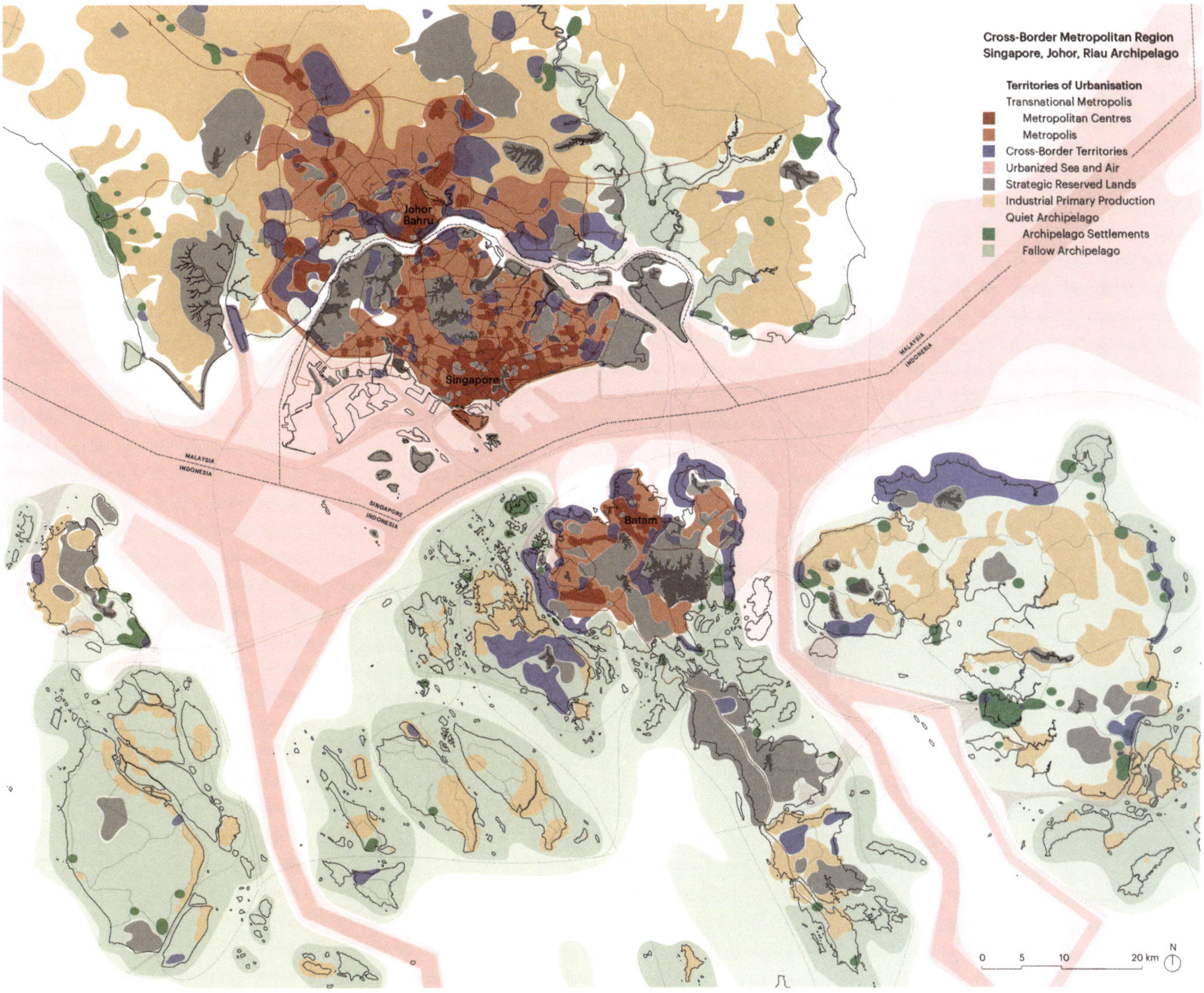

different scales, were put in focus. The investigation has revealed processes and procedures with which each of the resources is increasingly sought after by the city-state in a geopolitical frame, in the countries of the ASEAN and beyond. This increasing dependency on cross-border territories, ever further removed, is a source of vulnerability for Singapore. At the same time, these specific restrictions give a highly distinctive profile to Singapore's development practices, its urban character and form. Each of the five resource hinterlands has been described through maps, plans, diagrams and text, from the perspective of urban history, and in terms of socio-political, economic, and environmental development characteristics, with policy choices pursued.

The research does not represent the accustomed view of Singapore as an island developed on the paradigm of a global city-state, but as a city whose present and future are tightly connected to its cross border metropolitan region and the rest of South Asia.

A CONVERSATION W I T H Alberto Villanueva : Mars Utopia

Your project Mars Utopia embarks on creating an inhabitable territory on Mars using 3D printing. What does this concept involve?

This concept was developed with the idea of experimenting with new technologies to deal with the problem of overpopulation on Earth. One of the only possibilities for future years is to start developing new forms of architecture in extreme environments, or adapt our cities to future situations of extreme conditions.

If we are able to work with this technology in the most extreme environment known (with any possibility of life), in this case Mars, we would have the possibility to improve and develop this technology and techniques on Earth.

This project is the result of the freedom that generates an academic project. Everything started with the aim to push our imagination and skills to the limits of our knowledge.

Kerb:
Where on Mars would this be applied? How long would it take to create this new biosphere, and could humans roam freely without the need of Extravehicular Mobility Units (spacesuits)?

We have researched and simulated in different territories, from Hellas Planitia to the Gale Crater (Aeolis quadrangle). At this point in time we cannot disclose much more because it is part of a bigger research project that will be presented in the following months.

The first tests as part of my postgraduate research revealed that it could be possible to have a totally new stable biosphere in six years, but with first results after six months.

During the last few months, our university has been working with ESA and Science Museum designing spacesuits for the humans of the future who will live there. This has been a really interesting process where fashion, wearable technologies and science have merged. We need to think of how we can protect the humans living there until we reach a stable atmosphere there.

Kerb:
Would this new environment be considered artificial?

No, of course not. I know maybe for some people it could be because it is going against the established conditions, and we are modifying it. But we bear in mind that we want to recover the Mars of millions of years ago, where the possibility for our inhabitation could have been a real option.

What were the crucial phases in the testing processes? Was there any significant iteration?

There were many crucial phases. The first one was working out how to test the research in similar conditions, almost without resources. We commented before that this started as an academic project. The next phase was to work out how we can understand the territory. On Mars the scale is different, you can find valleys the depth of Everest. Our first question was if the architecture should adapt to the territory or to the needs of the future inhabitants, or if there was a possibility to find a balance and understand these interactions.

Understanding the 3D printing technology and adapting it to different environmental conditions was a crucial testing process. We studied how to adapt and generate new technologies to be controlled remotely. The experiments with different biological agents and new materials have been different crucial phases.

Inherent to any design process, setbacks arise that force us to consider alternative methods and/or directions. Did you encounter any difficulties that made you question if this is actually possible?

I encountered many difficulties. The main one was related to the impossibility of going to the place. One of the first lessons that you learn as an architect is the importance of visiting the site. Here it wasn't possible, and as a creative you lose the possibility to use your own sensations to understand the territory. But after internal fights and discussions with myself, I simply realised that you need to give that part to other professionals. I needed to be concentrating on the next steps. Use the information you have and apply it to achieve the goals.

Secondly, what was really difficult was the experimentation when I believed that I didn't have the biotechnological qualification to test and experiment with fungus, new materials and new technologies. But again, after many days of hard work I realised I have been preparing myself and training my mind and I just need to find a way to organise the elements to solve them. It has been like a puzzle. Every single time that I solved an issue, I had the sensation that I was creating another one.

The organisation and the ability to be working with several phases of the project at the same time have been part of the success of the project.

Could you elaborate on the collaboration between yourself, an architect/environmental designer, and NASA, who are more science focused? Was this a particularly challenging collaboration?

From the first moment we were considering the physical and environmental impact of the project, even we don't have any occupancy. Architecture is science. It requires rigor. The only difference between architecture and science is that architects' creative senses allow us to contemplate more needs than the fact of the numbers. We need to understand how 'strong' our towers are going to be.

This project has taught me the importance of multidisciplinary teams nowadays. Here was the challenge for me. As an architect educated in Spain and the UK, you think you can face any kind of challenge. It was less challenging than I expected. When you contemplate for the first time the possibility of having a discussion with brilliant minds around the world, it is overwhelming. But at the end of the day you are talking to people with similar qualifications and energies working for the best because they are trying to do the same as you, pursue excellence.

And as you have been in contact with NASA, is this actually going to happen? Why not tackle earth's extreme territories first?

I cannot confirm if it is going to happen. I am a small part of many groups of professionals and researchers working on these kinds of projects. Hopefully if all the testing continues in this direction there is the possibility.

Recently NASA tested one of the fungi proposed by us in space and it survived. As I commented before, the aim of this project is to help develop it in extreme environments on Earth. My goal is clear. But as in many kinds of these projects, only by thinking big are we going to be able to develop it.

Kerb:
Could a similar design intervention be applied on earth in the more extreme environments? Where would this be?

More than the 30 per cent of our territories are extreme or under the risk of becoming extreme environments. This intervention wants to create a dynamic and a structure that allows us recreate similar strategies on Earth.

For example, in our project the purpose of working with a fungus is to regenerate oxygen, it could be a good possibility to clean our atmosphere. We are contemplating a wide range of possibilities: the poles and deserts for example. KADK in Denmark or Lund School of Architecture have been good reference points, and they are following similar dynamics to us here, at Ravensbourne.

How has the issue of overpopulation influenced the way you practice design?

To be honest I started to contemplate this issue really late when I was designing my final major project based in the city of Seoul. I learnt a lot about that wonderful city and one of the details that really impressed me is how they were going to lose population in the following years in terms of a new sustainable design. But at the same time that made me reflect on the issue of overpopulation in Asia.

After that I started to collaborate with different online courses on the design of refugee camps, and there is when I started to realise the dimensions and the numbers of overpopulation.

Studying my second masters in Environment Design has provided me with a complete understanding of new techniques, materials and strategies focused in a new and necessary practice design.

What do you consider the notion of 'territory' to be, perhaps, from a futuristic perspective? How do you view this idea of territory in the context of your design?

Haesbaert makes a synthesis of the duality of territory and its components. 'Territory involves always at the same time... a symbolic, cultural dimension through a territory... an appropriation and spatial planning as a way of domain and discipline of individuals.' We discuss the appropriation of the space from a new point of view. We are not contemplating yet the human dimension, we are focused on the natural dimension.

The human being is the main disease of our planet Earth. We are responsible for the mistakes made. Many professionals approach this project thinking about how to adapt Mars to us. But Mars suffered a de-territorialisation millions of years ago, and we want to re-territorialise it in an environmental way. It must be viewed as a concomitant process, essential for a better understanding of human practices in the future.

From a futuristic perspective, territory is marked by one of the biggest problems of the modern society: time. We need to have it all as soon as possible, and this impetus has made many interesting projects based on the development of territory fail: Masdar, Silicon Valley, Tsukuba, Songdo, etc.

In the context of my design this could not be explained considering that we didn't want to show the exact points for the towers yet, or the new orography. As we discussed, the formation of a territory needs time. We need to have planning to avoid chaos; we shouldn't try to control more than the environment offers to us.

Was this concept of 'territory' significant from the beginning of your process? Was it a tool you worked with from the early conceptual stages or was it a developed product?

Yes, it was significant. One of my concerns is that nowadays we have simplified architecture to simple buildings. But architecture is much more than that. I was really interested in how to use it as an instrument for a more ambitious end. And if we think about Mars, the first thing to contemplate in our strategy is how to settle the territory.

During the first three months of this project I was basically trying to understand the geography, the composition; how the territory was formed and what was the real identity of what I had in front of me. Because of that I produced several models, 3D models, photomontages, sketches. It is not only about how to settle a tower. It is about how the growing of a life organism could be adapted to these specifications without damaging the identity of the planet.

Would you agree that 'territory' is a process rather than an outcome in terms of Mars Utopia?

It is a process and an outcome. At the beginning it was relevant to generate and use the resources available to adapt our needs to what the territories were offering to us. A process is not a discrete independent collection of elements, but interconnected landscapes with implications for the environment, such as climate, pollution or energy, and also for social and cultural spheres when we are thinking of the future. During this process we arrived at a point where the territory offers a solution and we can talk about an outcome.

As this is your project, if it came to be realised would you be tempted to move to Mars just to see it?

In an ideal situation, why not? But back to the reality, I never have contemplated that. But it is right that with all the advances and demonstrations of other professional teams, what started as the ambitious idea of an entrepreneur student has become a possibility.

Many times I have discussed with my colleagues these brave, and sometimes crazy, participants of the Mars ONE experience. They know they are not coming back to the Earth but they don't care about that. The experience is worth it.

MARS

MARS

TRAVERSING TERRITORIES

NORA AKAWI

In the epilogue of 'The Arab City: Architecture and Representation', political theorist and historian Timothy Mitchell proposes to "consider questions of meaning, signification, and representation that resist simple oppositions of the material and representational," and presents the possibility "to account for all of the ways that forms of inscription, forms of value, and forms of meaning are enfolded in every architectural work."[1]

In this text, Mitchell offers an approach to the history of the Arab city through the history of the corporation—the political-economic institution that has not only shaped modern cities, but that has also organised the relationship between the future and the present. He explains: "Through the business corporation, the building of cities can both create the future and appropriate it in the present. This power is simultaneously a question of materiality and of representation."[2] With 'The Arab City's' epilogue, and earlier with Mitchell's keynote lecture that followed the conference on which the book is based, the question of representation in architecture became inseparable from the relationship between the future and the present—the projection, imagination, appropriation, or the capitalisation of the future in the present.

As an extension of the efforts at Columbia University's GSAPP and its Studio-X Global Network to disrupt and challenge established canons in architecture education and introduce new territories into the research agenda of the school, The Arab City conference invited architects, urbanists, anthropologists, and historians from around the world to gather for a critical collective engagement with notions of identity, authenticity, and representation in architecture in the Arab Mashreq.[3] There were discussions on processes of fetishising, mimicking, essentialising, and 'othering' in architecture. There were also discussions on 'nested-Orientalism': the adoption of the image of one's self, people, or region as other, as it is drawn by the coloniser, and the reproduction of that image from within one's own culture. There were conversations on lost identities, lost modernities, and on the many aborted projects that were imagined for the future of Arab cities and streets. It was also an alarm against the dangerous yet common expectation of architecture to participate in the definition and production of national identity in projects of nation building, including those of Arab post-colonial nation-states. It was also an examination of the instances where architecture is instrumentalised to design particular forms of citizenship, to produce obedient and homogenised members of the nation, and to exclude, often violently, those who don't fit within it, those who struggle to be recognised in it and be represented by it. It was a call to understand architecture as a potentially "powerful marker of ambivalences, discontinuities, and instabilities."[4]
In her contribution to The Arab City, Felicity D. Scott urges us to "think of a type of post-nationalist figuration of architecture, a paradigm that refuses to collapse into, or even actively contests assumptions informing exclusivist notions like an Egyptian architecture, a Jordanian architecture, a Lebanese architecture, and so on."[5] In addition to considering architecture's role in colonial projects and in nation-building projects in the Arab region, the conference and book also address architecture's participation in the extermination of identities and cultures, and ask: which are the forces that have shaped the dominant representations in architecture in the Arab World and which are the representations that have been silenced or erased in the process, and why? Why were they understood as threats? What is their power? And what is their claim against the narratives of dominating powers and authority? How do we excavate their stories? And how do we construct our own, with these struggles in mind?

Thinking about construction, about the future, in times as dark as these, not only for our own region but for all other of the parts of the world that are being considered as disposable, is a difficult task. Naomi Klein recently gave an address at the Edward Said lecture in London about Orientalism, climate change violence, and environmental

Xiaoxi Chen, 'Earthworks, Borders, and In-Between Settlements' from the course 'Echoing Borders' (taught by Nora Akawi and Nina V. Kolowratnik at Columbia University GSAPP, Fall 2014). In this mapping and essay project, Xiaoxi Chen investigates the No-Man's Land on the Syrian-Jordanian border (the Syrian-Jordanian Neutral Zone). She focused in particular on the zone around Rubkan from July to November 2014, as it transformed from an informal crossing point over the trenches of sand into a formalised and militarised crossing point and camp (where a few thousand refugees from Syria where held as Jordan was closing its borders, but where today over 70,000 people wait in extremely peculiar conditions).

Opposite top:
Syrian Jordan Border Neutral Zone

Opposite middle:
Movement Tracking in Rubkan Border Neutral Zone:
July – November 2014

Opposite bottom:
Probable In Place Settlement in Rubkan Border Neutral Zone:
July – November 2014

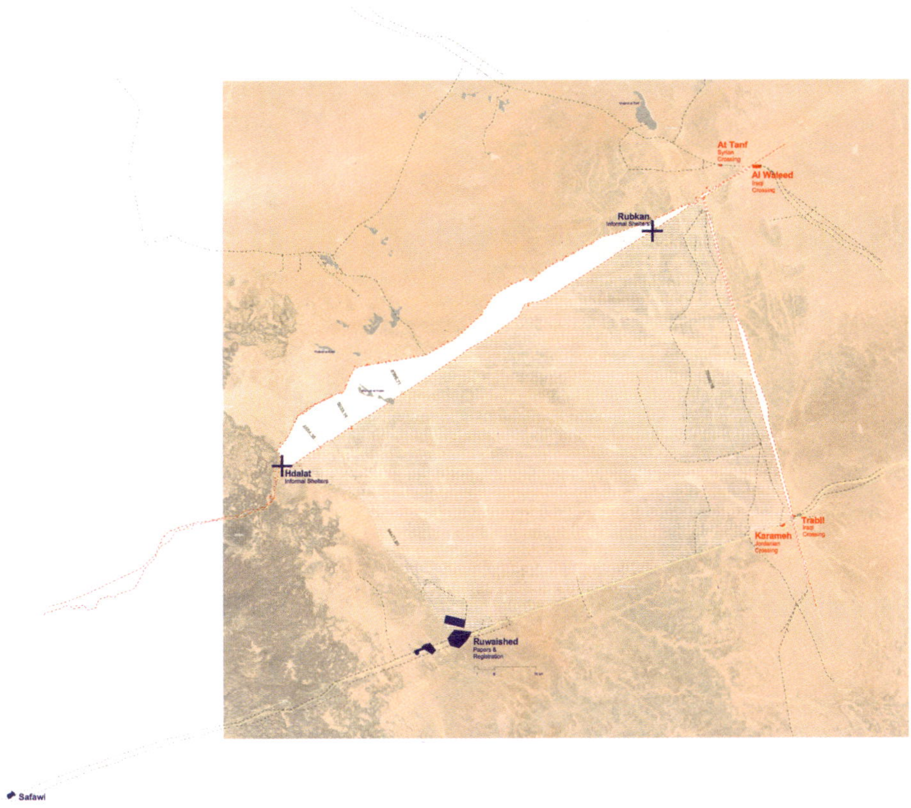
At Tanf
Syrian Crossing
Al Waleed
Iraqi Crossing
Rubkan
Informal Shelters
Hdalat
Informal Shelters
Trabil
Iraqi Crossing
Karameh
Jordanian Crossing
Ruwaished
Papers & Registration
Safawi

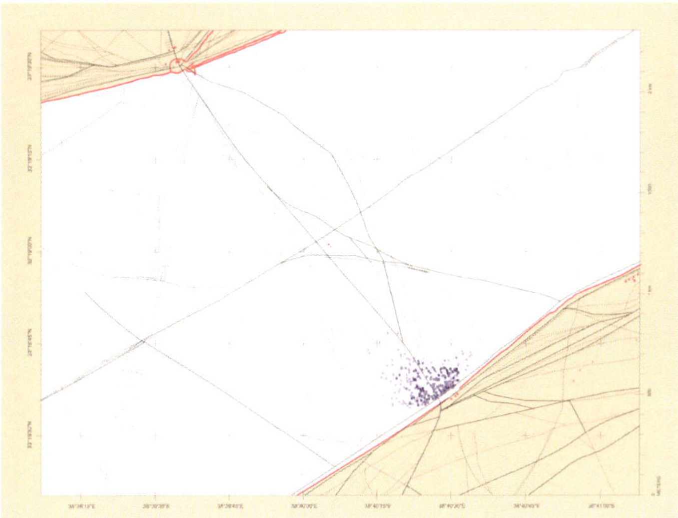

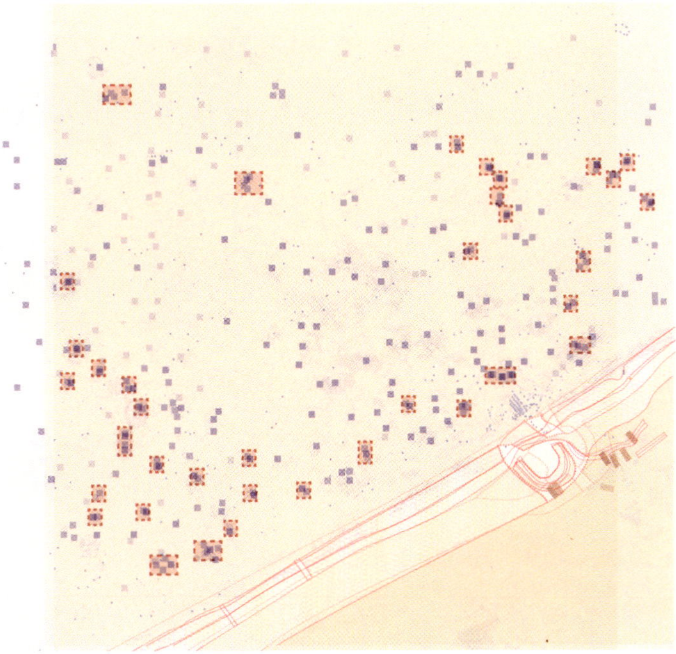

racism. She started with the recognition that Said was no tree hugger. He was less interested in the claims of tree huggers, particularly when he compared their struggle with that of those fighting against direct violent threats of expulsion, of erasure, of execution. But in this lecture, Klein reminds us that the transgressions that are executed against parts of the world (occupation, expulsion, destruction, including environmental violence against regions, livelihoods, and cultures) wouldn't have been possible without orders of systemic racism like Orientalism, a form of 'othering' (the disregarding, essentialising and denuding of the humanity of another people or region).[6] She explains that the reckless refusal of governments to take action and responsibility in regard to the climate crisis wouldn't have been possible without institutional racism. This recklessness wouldn't have been possible without Orientalism, and other theories of human hierarchy-the tools that allow for the sacrifice of zones of the globe, and the sacrifice of the rights, the bodies, and cultures of those who inhabit them. The othering of territories and cultures 'softens the ground' for transgression (violent expulsion, land theft, occupation, invasion), and cannot be separated from the systems of colonialism, capitalism, privatisation, militarism, and the environmental racism that it supports.[7]

In the context of architecture studies, it's important to recognise that this violence, this othering doesn't happen far away in unfamiliar places. Practices of othering happen in educational and cultural institutions like the ones we work for and with, including our universities. With the important link that Klein makes between Orientalism (and other forms of othering) and environmental racism, we can see the violence we witness against populations condemned to a lower rank in the diagrams of human hierarchy as clear testimony that such institutions (academic and other) have not yet succeeded in ridding themselves of practices of othering. In one of the major engines of othering, the academic institution, the cultures and places of those condemned to a lower rank in the human hierarchy, if they are recognized at all, are exoticised, flattened, and often taught and researched as problems in need of a solution. Architecture studies in Israeli academic institutions in Jerusalem are a noteworthy example. Jerusalem is a city that is being shaped by the state's systemic racism and urban violence against Palestinians through segregation, destruction, urban suffocation, expulsion, policing, even execution. With that, it is possible to go through five years of studio and seminar courses in professional architecture studies in Jerusalem without setting foot in Palestinian space, and without mention of Palestinian history or culture, except for a class where a particular Israeli architectural style is explained as having found its inspiration in Arab architecture—an orientalist approach to history that uproots Palestinian architectural production from its political and cultural lineage, and renders it as an empty signifier which in this case is made to carry with it an image of Israeli belonging to the land. This theft (of politics, of indigenous culture, of memory and, as a result, of possible futures) is one of the forms of violent 'othering' that architecture curricula continue to participate in worldwide. This form of violence is not only a deliberate denial and ignorance of different stories of our shared world but an eternal silencing of other imaginaries for it. It is an active complacency, a facilitation of the transgression that such stories, their authors, and their spaces are made to endure. Unless we continuously and actively work to challenge those who constitute the walls of the colonial-euro-American-white-centric canon, we become complicit through knowledge and cultural production that allow for forms of systemic racism that in turn makes it possible to sacrifice people and their environments for the benefit of a few. It's with this level of urgency that Naomi Klein calls for the joining of forces against injustice, because struggles against othering, racism, occupation, expulsion, and environmental violence can no longer be understood and fought separately.

In 'Identity, Authority, and Freedom: The Potentate and the Traveler', a lecture Edward Said delivered at the University of Cape Town in South Africa in 1991, he addresses the still very pressing question of academic freedom—the privileges but also the social and political responsibilities of civic institutions like the university, as well as the dangers of the relationship between the university and national identity. Said argues that "[to] make the practice of intellectual discourse dependent on conformity to a predetermined political ideology,"

1. Mitchell, T. (2016). The Captial City. In Andraos, A., Akawi, N., & Blanchfield, C (Eds), The Arab City: Architecture and Representation. New York: Columbia Books on Architecture and the City. p258.

2. Ibid.

3. 'The Arab City: Architecture and Representation' conference was co-curated by Amale Andraos and Nora Akawi, and held on November 21st, 2014 at Columbia University's Graduate School of Architecture, Planning, and Preservation in partnership with Columbia University's Middle East Institute and the Columbia Global Centers | Amman.

4. Scott, F.D. (2016). Architecture and Nation Building. In Andraos, A., Akawi, N., & Blanchfield, C (Eds), The Arab City: Architecture and Representation. New York: Columbia Books on Architecture and the City. p139.

5. Ibid.

6. Naomi Klein, 'Let Them Drown: The Violence of Othering in a Warming World' initially delivered as the Edward Said London Lecture and later published in the London Review of Books (Vol. 38, No. 11, June 2016, pp11-14). She adds that "the project of Orientalism, of othering Arab and Muslim people, has been the silent partner of our oil dependence from the start – and inextricable, therefore, from the blowback that is climate change. If nations and peoples are regarded as other – exotic, primitive, bloodthirsty, as Said documented in the 1970s – it is far easier to wage wars and stage coups when they get the crazy idea that they should control their own oil in their own interests."

7. Ibid.

8 Said, E. (2000). Identity, Authority, and Freedom: The Potentate and the Traveler. Reflections on Exile and Other Essays. Cambridge: Harvard University Press. p396.

9. Ibid, emphasis added.

10. Roy, A. (2009). 'The 21st Century Metropolis: New Geographies of Theory'. Regional Studies, 43.6. p820.

11. Ibid, p821.

12. Amin, A. (2004). Regions Unbound: Towards a New Politics of Place. Geografiska Annaler: Series B, Human Geography 86. pp33-44.

13. Roy, 'The 21st Century Metropolis: New Geographies of Theory' (2009), p821, emphasis added.

14. Mathias, A., Jacobson, D., & Lapid, Y. (2001). Identities, Borders, Orders: Rethinking International Relations Theory. University of Minnesota Press.

or predetermined canon of learning, Western or other, "is to nullify intellect altogether."[8] For him, academic freedom is the freedom to be critical, the rejection of any kind of homely comfort:

"The world we live in is made up of numerous identities interacting, sometimes harmoniously, sometimes antithetically. Not to deal with that whole is not to have academic freedom. We cannot make our claim as seekers after justice if we advocate knowledge only of and about ourselves. Our model for academic freedom should therefore be the migrant or the traveler: for if, in the real world outside the academy, we must be ourselves and only ourselves, inside the academy we should be able to discover and travel among other selves, other identities, other varieties of the human adventure."[9]

In 'The 21st Century Metropolis: New Geographies of Theory', Ananya Roy urges us to rethink the geographies of urban and regional theory, to "blast open theoretical geographies," which "requires 'dislocating' the EuroAmerican centre of theoretical production." She writes that "it is not enough simply to study the cities of the global South as interesting, anomalous, different, and esoteric empirical cases. Such forms of benign difference making keep alive the neo-orientalist tendencies that interpret Third World cities as the heart of darkness, the Other."[10] Roy recalls[11] Ash Amin's 'Regions Unbound: Toward a New Politics of Place'[12] where he proposes "a 'relational' or 'topological' reading of regions, such that the local is viewed as a 'field of agonistic engagement' with 'different scales of politics/social action". Roy's essay expands on Amin's call for a relational reading of territories, and invites us to join an agenda for the study of the 21st century metropolis through the production of theory in the global South that is "focused on a variety of dynamic topologies and deep relationalities: the worlding of cities, the production and politics of space, and exurbanity and extraterritoriality."[13]

The interest in terms like worlding used in Roy's proposal for new regional and urban theory is shared by writers on international relations theory who borrow the practice of verbing from communication studies. In the book Identities, Borders, Orders: Rethinking International Relations Theory, the editors critique international relations theory as it is still largely based on "stability, continuity, and territorial sovereignty as a master ordering principle," which they consider insufficient for the study and theory of relations that are constantly in formation.[14] They refer to communication theorist Brenda Dervin's question "how does one focus on moves when all one has is nouns with which to work?"[15] They propose processual, relational and verbing modes of thinking as a way of grasping identities, borders and orders that are constantly 'in-formation' and 'in-relation'. In response, international relations scholars have worked with terms like bordering,[16] securitizing,[17] and refugeeing.[18]

Similarly, Ananya Roy's 'New Geographies of Theory' borrows from authors proposing to rethink area studies, particularly Arjun Appadurai's proposal to shift the emphasis from 'trait geographies' to 'process geographies':[19] "in other words, on the forms of movement, encounter, and exchange that confound the idea of bounded world-regions with immutable traits." She proposes thinking through 'process geographies' can help forge new geographies of urban theory.[20]

'Echoing Borders', a mapping and research project initiated through Studio-X Amman at Columbia University's GSAPP, situates itself at the tension between the rising intensity of migration across borders on the one hand, and on the other the still fixed understandings and representations of territories and their boundaries and the static definition of citizenship and human rights.[21]

The concept of sovereignty emerged from the efforts to push out others from a territory, efforts driven by fear. The term territory is derived from the fifteenth's century French term terrier (to frighten or to terrorize). The term's original etymology was displaced in the eighteenth century by the Latin term territorium which combines terra (land) and thorium (belonging to, or surrounding). With the role of sovereignty as that which overcomes a territory's 'other' organisation, territory was then haunted by the fear of the other. In other words, the 'other' was what the sovereign aimed to displace, in its role as the controller or organiser of space. In international law, sovereignty is "the control of a well defined territory,"

15. Dervin, B. (1993). Verbing Communication: Mandate for Disciplinary Invention.Journal of Communication, 43(4), p45.

16. Albert, M., & Brock, L. (1996). Debordering the world of states: New spaces in international relations. New Political Science, 18(1), 69-106.

17. Waever, O. (1995). International relations -- The New European Security Disorder by Simon Duke. The American Political Science Review, 89(3), 798.

18. Soguk, N. (1999). States and strangers: Refugees and displacements of statecraft. Minneapolis: University of Minnesota Press.

19. Appadurai, A. (2000). Grassroots Globalization and the Research Imagination.Public Culture, 12. pp1-19.

20. Roy, A. (2009). The 21st-Century Metropolis: New Geographies of Theory. Regional Studies, 43(6), p821.

21. The project 'Echoing Borders' was initiated in 2014 by Nora Akawi and Nina V. Kolowratnik at the Graduate School of Architecture, Planning and Preservation (GSAPP) at Columbia University through an annual Fall seminar course, research travel, and summer workshop.

22. Gottsman, J. (1973). The Significance of Territory. Charlottesville: University Press of Virginia.

23. Jennings, R.Y. (1963). The Acquisition of Territory in International Law. Manchester: Manchester University Press.

24. Scott, F. (1932). 'The Island of Palmas' in Hague Court Reports.

25. Benhabib, S. (2004). The Rights of Others: Aliens, Residents, and Citizens. Cambridge University Press. p6.

26. Nora Akawi and Nina V. Kolowratnik, 'Echoing Borders' syllabus, Columbia University GSAPP, Fall 2015.

27. Said, E. (1991). Identity, Authority, and Freedom: The Potentate and the Traveler. Transition, (54), p404.

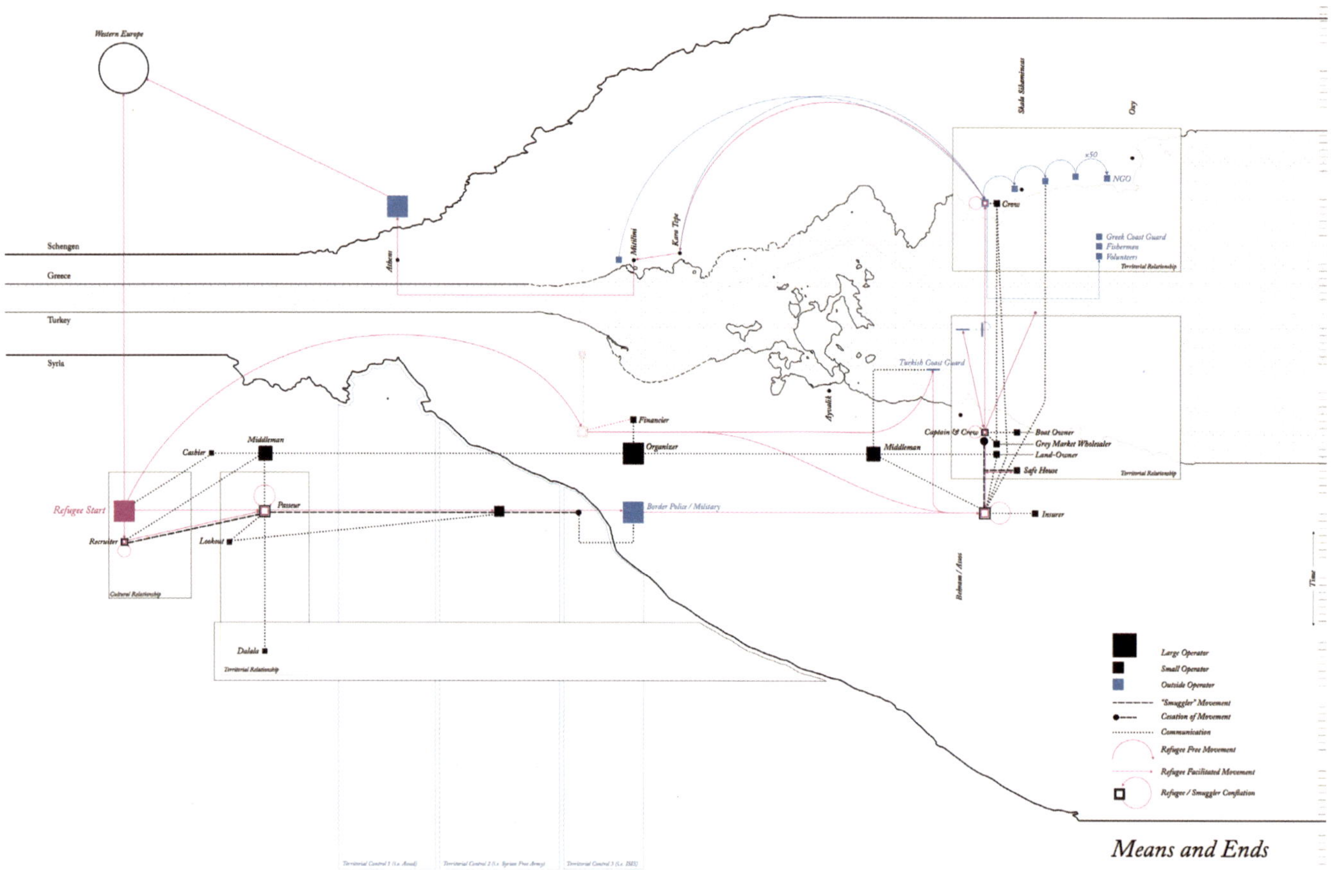

Means and Ends

and territory designates the land "under the jurisdiction of a sovereign."[22] Also, according to the law, a sovereign state could acquire territory through "an act of effective apprehension, such as occupation or conquest."[23] Map-making and boundary-marking became the way to establish sovereignty over a territory. The law stated that "states may, by convention, fix limits to their own sovereignty, even in regions such as the interior of scarcely explored continents where such sovereignty is scarcely manifested, and in this way each may prevent the other from any penetration of its territory."[24]

In the introduction to 'The Rights of Others: Aliens, Residents, and Citizens', Seyla Benhabib writes that "[the] old political structures may have waned but the new political forms of globalisation are not yet in sight. We are like travelers navigating an unknown terrain with the help of old maps, drawn at a different time and in response to different needs. While the terrain we are traveling on, the world society of states, has changed, our normative map has not."[25] Mappings and essays developed through the 'Echoing Borders' initiative aim at identifying and representing ambivalences and discontinuities, as proposed by Felicity D. Scott, of seemingly defined and uncontestable territories and border lines. The project takes as a starting point our understanding of territoriality that is still heavily rooted in our imagination of the world as divided into compartmentalised, distinct, and mutually exclusive formations. As stated in the 'Echoing Borders' syllabus, "considering that borders are physically manifested through fences and trenches, but also through biometric identification technology, refugee registration offices, (in)access to jobs and healthcare, and fluctuating policies and regulations. The project attempts to redraw contemporary borders with focus

Jason Danforth, 'Means and Ends' from the course "Echoing Borders" (taught by Nora Akawi and Nina V. Kolowratnik at Columbia University GSAPP, Fall 2015). As both a research paper and cartographic exercise, Jason Danforth's project seeks to problematise the image of the smuggler as a singular, monolithic figure by identifying the many roles and individuals which comprise the sprawling web of smuggling networks. Operating under the model of Bruno Latour, this project is an attempt to 'draw things together', and represent the complex cultural, economic, and territorial figure(s) of the smuggler and their relationship to the current migration crisis spanning the Middle East and Europe.

"...[the] old political structures may have waned but the new political forms of globalisation are not yet in sight. We are like travelers navigating an unknown terrain with the help of old maps, drawn at a different time and in response to different needs. While the terrain we are traveling on, the world society of states, has changed, our normative map has not."

- Ananya Roy

As the response to the Syrian migrant crisis has grown more complex, extending beyond early, more explicitly humanitarian relief efforts, to include a variety of exploitative, profit-driven enterprises, legal scholars have once again turned their attention to the problematic line that separates smuggling from human trafficking. The networks that facilitate the movement of bodies across traditional borders have swelled as numerous thirdparty actors have entered the field, further problematising an already questionable dichotomy, and with it the legal repercussions for those forced to rely upon these networks to reach safety.

on elements of movement and time - shifting away from the conventional, static representations of what are in fact dynamic and unstable conditions. As political theorists suggest that the figure of the refugee is central to contemporary politics, the project aims to visualise migration and movement across borders, both regular and irregular, recognised and unrecognised, as the central elements that define contemporary territories and geopolitical terrains. The project mobilises familiar visualisation attributes and activates them not as static representations, but as processes in themselves; not to be taken as technologies of capture, but as techniques of addition, drawing and critically investigating processes of bordering."[26] The hope is that rather than reading borderlands as fixed and static conditions, through a critical analysis and representation of processes of both fabricating and dismantling borders, new imaginaries for territories can emerge.

In Edward Said's critical essay on academic freedom 'Identity, Authority, and Freedom', he writes that there are two ways of inhabiting the academic institution. The first is the academic professional who is there in order to reign: the king or the potentate who surveys everything with detachment and authority. This entails dictating what should and should not be taught, what should or should not be included, defining disciplinary boundaries, reinforcing existing canons. The second is based on the figure of the migrant, "considerably more mobile, more playful, although no less serious. The image of the traveler depends not on power but on motion, on a willingness to go into different masks and rhetorics.... Most of all, and most unlike the potentate who must guard only one place and defend its frontiers, the traveler crosses over, traverses territory, and abandons fixed positions, all the time."[27]

A CONVERSATION WITH Saskia Sassen: Expulsions

What impact has the globalisation and privatisation of trade, laws and economies, had on our understanding of territory? Have global corporations become new nation-states unto themselves?

I don't think I would put the bit on corporations in those terms. For one, they have a state – 'our' states, so to speak. Why bother with the hard work of inventing and running one. Our states have been key handmaidens in the current transformation. As for your question on territory, I see the current era as including a type of imperialism that is quite different from the earlier Western imperial modes and from the post WWII Keynesian driven capitalism which existed well into the 1980s. I see new systemic logics arising from the decaying political economy of the twentieth century…and these include expulsion logics to a far larger and more extreme extent than the preceding Keynesian period, which also had some of this, but not as widespread. This decay began in the 1980s. By then the strong welfare states and workers' syndicates established in much of the West, including several Latin American countries, had either been devastated or were under severe pressure. To some extent, state projects, with people-oriented welfare programs, had also been strong features in other parts of the world, including, in their own ways, communist countries and those with varieties of socialist nationalism, as illustrated by Nasser's welfare-state policies in Egypt, systems developed in several post-independence African countries, and in India's brand of state socialism. In these countries too, decay began in the 1980s and 1990s.

To talk of this decay is not to romanticize the twentieth century, a period marked by devastating wars, genocides, and starvation, and by extreme ideologies of both left and right. When I speak of traditional capitalism it is to shorthand the era dominated by mass consumption, when this is the sector that is the key organizer of capitalism (and hence the higher the consumption capacity of individuals, households, governments, and firms) the better for the system overall. This sector brought on a vast expansion of those who were incorporated into the system. This was an economic phase where the broad middle—from the working class to the modest middle class—expanded rapidly. The construction of suburban housing and infrastructure meant a sharp increase in the demand for an enormous range of goods. The expansion of the demand for automobiles meant the vast expansion of road, tunnel, and bridge building. The U.S. is the most extreme case certainly, partly given the very physical fact of its vast territory, but we see this dynamic also in Europe and Latin America and in parts of Africa, as well as in Communist Russia.

Kerb:
So where does that leave traditional governance?

The space of traditional governance is shrinking, even though it remains the most strategically important and powerful. What is expanding is a vast new zone of ambiguous rules and 'ruling orders'. The rules range widely – from private formal arrangements, such as international commercial arbitration, which bypasses national courts, to the agreements among a growing number of international criminal syndicates. And the 'ruling orders' range from terrorists organisations to large global firms with the power to shape much of the global economy.

The overall outcome of this redrawing of global inter-state space is a multiplication of systemic edges - and these do not correspond to national borders or the formal inter-state system. The most extreme case is probably ISIS and its 'Caliphate'.

But we can see many less extreme and less belligerent formations if our aim is to identify new kinds of enclosures that partly disassemble national sovereign territory and thereby unsettle the traditional inter-state system. In my own work I have focused on a range of such enclosures. Among them are commercial land grabs - shorthand for massive land acquisitions by firms and governments in countries not their own; these have reached well over 200 million hectares from 2006 to 2011. Another instance is the so-called 'black pools of finance' (as described by Bernanke, the former head of the US central bank[1]); these are mostly electronic spaces that cut across national borders, and have territorial insertions in key countries and global cities. They are run by major established banks, and account for a growing share of financial transactions but fall outside the standard regulatory frame.

Finally, and more diffuse, the rise of inter-city relations across national borders will keep on expanding, which I explored in my piece on emergent urban geopolitics, 'The Future of the City'.[2] Elsewhere I have examined how this is in good part, and perhaps ironically, a result of governments implementing economic deregulation and privatisation policies (see my Cities in a World Economy, 4th updated edition, Sage 2012). These took off in the Global North in the 1980s and have now spread in one version or another to much of the world.

What do you see as the social or local impact of this?

Devastating, brutal, unacceptable.

The dominant logic is one of extraction. This is what I examine and elaborate on in Expulsions, and why I found that only looking at inequality is not enough. Thus I find that even finance, which looks so very non-extractive, is actually marked by a logic of extraction. This is quite different from traditional banking, more dominated by the logic of mass consumption: the more the better, and the better the sons and daughters do, the better. Today this is quite secondary to the system, even though not to the ongoing mass consumption bit. But it does also contribute to explain why the 'system' has allowed so much of the prosperous working class and modest middle classes to become poorer.

In my more contemplative moments, my take for now is that we need the complex apparatus that is a working state. In principle the state should contain the major conflictive alignments: the labor department should combat the finance department for social justice to workers; the national economic department should contest the global affairs department so that the country does not lose too much - say via the new types of trade agreements (which are really investment agreements: they give investors all kinds of securities and capacity to sue states if something goes wrong). I have dealt with a lot of this in my book Territory, Authority, Rights.

A working state is a complex capability that can factor in multiple interests and perspectives - it has multiple vectors or sectors - some are disastrous, truly evil, others are great for activists who want justice, for the environmental struggle, etc. It should help us to bring into the political discussion a whole range of perspectives that are critical, often very concrete, generated by the specifics of a region, a labor union's struggle, claims by poor students, a local economy - for instance, a local economy dominated by large international mining companies is going to be very different from one controlled by a small middle class business sector.

A very different case of added knowledge that a working state can enable is represented by the critical literature that emerged in India under the name of the subaltern. It added a lot to our understanding of the old empires of the nineteenth and eighteenth centuries. I am sure that in countries such as Iran and Pakistan, where there are major scholars and schools of thought, you have yet other contributions to a critical analysis. I see this also as a very specific vector that enables us to make visible in a region, in a country, across countries, a whole variety of the very specifically located issues. That is good. We (those without power) can use this, it becomes a capability in our hands. The question then becomes, what do we do with it?

In 'Visible Formations and Formally Visible Facticities' you state that '...the twentieth century saw the strengthening of alignment between territory and territoriality. But the past two decades have once again brought about more misalignments, some recognized and some not.' Would you care to expand on this in our current global setting?

I am so glad you found this article since it is in a law journal, quite removed from the social sciences. I have found myself giving quite a few talks in law schools and writing pieces in law journals

What I described in that article is a first little step towards the current project 'Ungoverned Territories?' The focus is on the territorial...moving away from the standard category 'national sovereign territory'. I ask questions such as 'are the vast stretches of dead land the terrae nullius of our epoch?'

There is a more recent, far more developed version that was part of my Storrs Lectures in Philosophy and Jurisprudence, at the Yale University Law School. It is called 'When Territory De-borders Territoriality.' I wonder whether this title is clear to you. It represents an inversion of the common notion that often the authority (territoriality) of the state seeks to go beyond its territorial borders – with powerful countries such as the US and Russia the most dramatic examples.

In Expulsions you talk about foreign land ownership as an 'invisible' conquest of national territory. A 'partial denationalization deep inside nation-states'. Do you see the acquisition of land by foreign nations and multinational corporations as being as dangerous in diminishing sovereign authority of the state over its own territory, as say, imperial conquests of the past?

I see it as a radically different mode: one key difference is that there is no super-structural project. As the project, for instance of the Brits in India to generate a proper bureaucratic professional class, the subaltern, or the project of the French, the mission civilisatrice, teaching all members of the empire French, proper French. Today, the land grabs are just an instance of extraction. The Chinese have made this the clearest because when they acquire land or mines (or whatever) they bring their workers, build hospitals (since their workers cannot handle the climate), build roads, harbours, bridges to secure the outcome. And when they are done extracting, they leave, and they leave it all behind. This is what I mean by the absence of a super-structural project. Whether it is better or worse for the countries involved...I don't know, but it certainly also includes a lot of devastated land and water. It is not benign. It is just different. For me the language of extraction works better than the so much used 'imperial'.

Kerb:
What is the role of the nation-state in all of this?

One brief observation that I have researched in my work on global cities is the following: when a government deregulates and privatises economic sectors (once under the direct management of the state), these managerial and regulatory functions do not disappear. They are transferred to private firms: they reappear as specialised financial, accounting, legal, advisory services for corporations. And these types of activities tend to be in cities, and in global cities if they are complex because a firm's market is global.

None of this eliminates the ongoing role of the inter-state system and its multiple institutions. Indeed, some of these have become more important and are entering new domains. Let me illustrate this with what is an obscure event, the so-called 'vulture funds' issue in the Argentine sovereign default. What had been the domain of narrow court procedures became a matter of interest and active engagement for the General Assembly of the United Nations in the Fall of 2014, a process that continues,[3] and yet, none of this can obliterate the fact of that expanding global space of ambivalent new rules and new ruling orders.

You speak of your point of inquiry in Expulsions as being the systemic edge, how do you define this edge condition?

The key dynamic at this edge is expulsion from the diverse systems in play – economic, social, biospheric. This edge is foundationally different from notions such as social exclusion: these happen inside the system and supposedly proper policy could change or reduce the damage. It is also foundationally different from the geographic border in the interstate system. The focus on the edge comes from one of the core hypotheses organising this book: that the move from Keynesianism to the global era of privatisations, deregulation, and open borders for some, entailed a switch from dynamics that brought people into the economic system (via mass consumption, hence the interest of economic sectors to have the state enable the middle classes with various supports) to dynamics that push people out.

These expulsion logics are also evident beyond the West, as I argue particularly in the long chapter on environmental destruction, 'Dead Land Dead Water'. Determining whether such a switch from incorporation to expulsion might also be emerging in countries that have had high growth rates (even if now falling), such as China and India, requires expertise I lack. China, especially, has seen a massive incorporation of people into monetised economies, but now many of these are among the growing masses of 'monetised' poor! China is also experiencing sharpening inequality and new forms of economic concentration at the top, not to mention corporate bullying.

Each major domain has its own distinctive systemic edge (constituted differently for say the economy than for the biosphere). One of the organising assumptions in this book is that the systemic edge is the site where general, familiar (not monstrous or weird, but the usual, the familiar!) conditions take extreme forms precisely because it is the site for expulsion. Further, the extreme character of conditions at the edge helps us detect more encompassing trends that are less extreme and hence more difficult to capture. I conceive of these larger trends as conceptually subterranean because we cannot easily make them visible through our current categories of meaning.

Would you say that international borders still matter?

Yes, for some...especially that which is made by flesh and bones. But not for many cross-border flows. Let me elaborate, as this is one of my pet subjects... I have been working on this alternative understanding about the role for borders for the last ten years. So let me indulge...

State sovereignty is usually understood as the state's monopoly of authority over a particular territory, demarcated by reasonably established geographic borders. Today, it is becoming evident that even as national territories remain bounded by traditional geographic borderlines, globalisation is causing novel types of 'borderings' to multiply; these borderings range from regimes protecting firms' trading rights (even when incompatible with domestic law in signatory countries) to emerging forms of protections for threatened species whose habitats comprise more than one country. These novel borderings cut across traditional borders and become evident both globally and inside national territory. Sovereignty remains a systemic property; that is to say, the interstate and supranational systems remain dependent on the presence and recognition of the mutually exclusive authority of national states over their territories, even when the International Monetary Fund (IMF), World Trade Organization (WTO) law, or the jurisdiction of the International Criminal Court (ICC) have chipped away at that exclusivity.

The institutional space for sovereignty now includes specific functions and authorities of these global institutions. This, in turn, chips away at the State's capacity to legitimate –through the legislature, the courts and executive decree, or by signing on to international treaties. Although weak, these diverse emergent regimes cut into the foundational proposition of the exclusive authority of the State over its territory. The politics of sovereignty now include claims for sovereignty on the part of Indigenous people, today recognised by at least some states (notably Canada), as well as claims by global regulators seeking to override particular aspects of state sovereignty, notably through WTO law and IMF conditionality in the 1980s and 1990s. The outcomes are more complex than notions of mutually exclusive territorial authority can capture.

1. Sassen, S. (2014). Expulsions : Brutality and complexity in the global economy. Cambridge MA: Harvard University Press. Chaper 3

2. Sassen, S. (2013). The Future of the City: Ephemeral Kingdoms, Eternal Cities. The European Magazine. Retrieved from http://www.theeuropean-magazine.com/saskia-sassen--3/6573-the-future-of-the-city

3. Sassen, S., Owens, L. (2014). The Vultures of Wall Street: The Financial Firms that Prey on Sovereign Debt. Boston Review. Retrieved from http://bostonreview.net/world/lisa-lucile-owens-saskia-sassen-vulture-funds

CITY OF SEVEN BILLION

JOYCE HSIANG & BIMAL MENDIS: PLAN B ARCHITECTURE & URBANISM

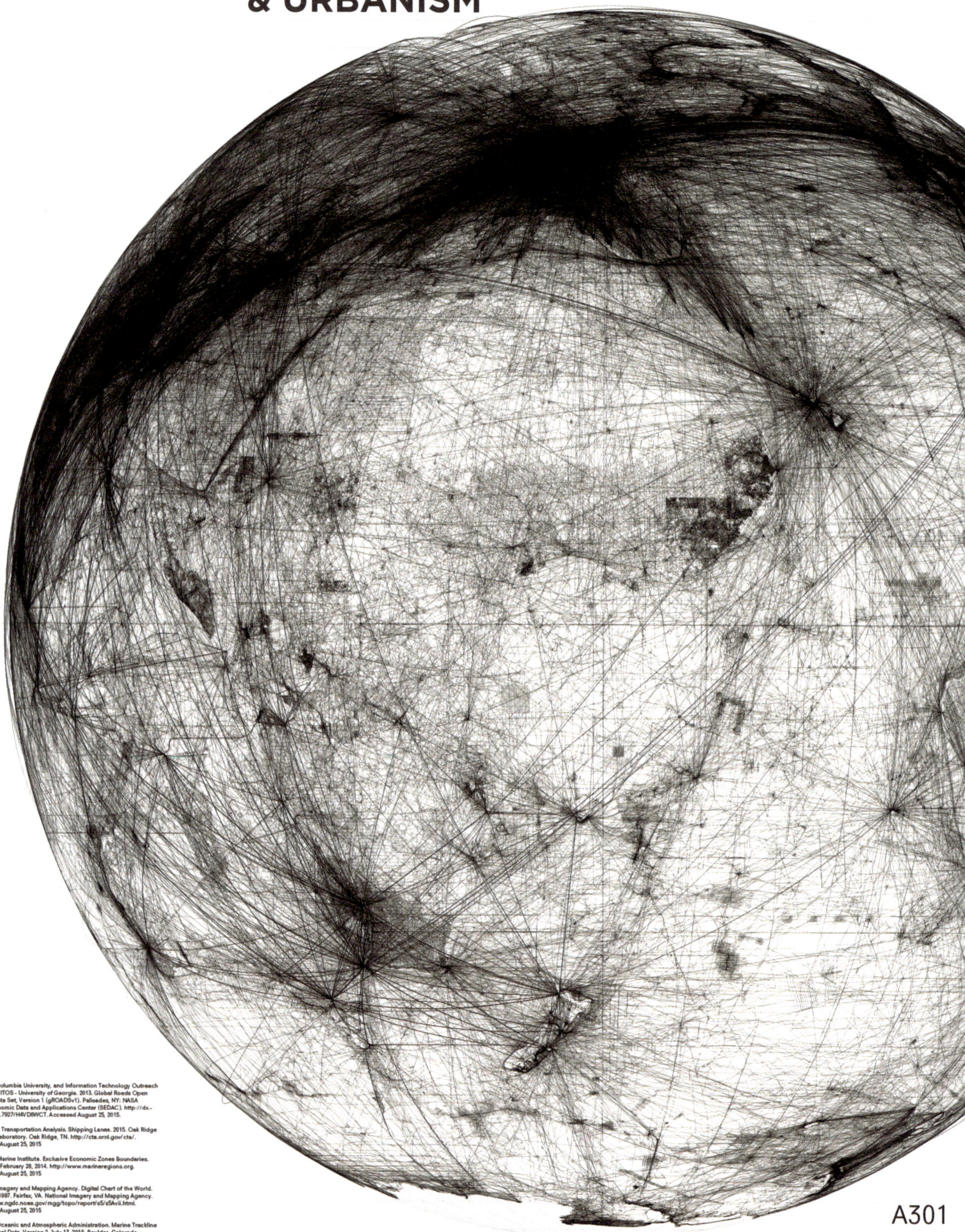

CIESIN - Columbia University, and Information Technology Outreach Services - ITOS - University of Georgia. 2013. Global Roads Open Access Data Set, Version 1 (gROADSv1). Palisades, NY: NASA Socioeconomic Data and Applications Center (SEDAC). http://dx.-doi.org/10.7927/H4VD6WCT. Accessed August 25, 2015.

Center for Transportation Analysis. Shipping Lanes. 2015. Oak Ridge National Laboratory. Oak Ridge, TN. http://cta.ornl.gov/cta/. Accessed August 25, 2015

Flanders Marine Institute. Exclusive Economic Zones Bounderies. Version 8. February 28, 2014. http://www.marineregions.org. Accessed August 25, 2015

National Imagery and Mapping Agency. Digital Chart of the World. Edition 3. 1997. Fairfax, VA. National Imagery and Mapping Agency. http://www.ngdc.noaa.gov/mgg/topo/report/s5/s5Avii.html. Accessed August 25, 2015

National Oceanic and Atmospheric Administration. Marine Trackline Geophysical Data. Version 2. July 13, 2015. Boulder, Colorado. https://www.ngdc.noaa.gov/mgg/geodas/trackline.html. Accessed August 25, 2015

OpenFlights. Flight Paths. August 25, 2015. Content Share. Singa-pore,Malaysia. http://openflights.org. Accessed August 25, 2015.

TeleGeography. Submarine Cable Map. 2015. Washington, D.C. August 25, 2015. http://www.submarinecablemap.com. Accessed August 25, 2015.

A301

HE HAD BOUGHT A LARGE MAP REPRESENTING THE SEA, WITHOUT THE LEAST VESTIGE OF LAND: AND THE CREW WERE MUCH PLEASED FOR THEY FOUND IT TO BE A MAP THEY COULD ALL UNDERSTAND.

"WHAT'S THE GOOD OF MERCATOR'S NORTH POLES AND EQUATORS, TROPICS, ZONES AND MERIDIAN LINES?" SO THE BELLMAN WOULD CRY: AND THE CREW WOULD REPLY "THEY ARE MERELY CONVENTIONAL SIGNS!

OTHER MAPS AND SUCH SHAPES, WITH THEIR ISLANDS AND CAPES! BUT WE'VE GOT OUR BRAVE CAPTAIN TO THANK: (SO THE CREW WOULD PROTEST) "THAT HE'S BOUGHT US THE BEST - A PERFECT AND ABSOLUTE BLANK!"

- THE HUNTING OF THE SNARK, LEWIS CARROLL

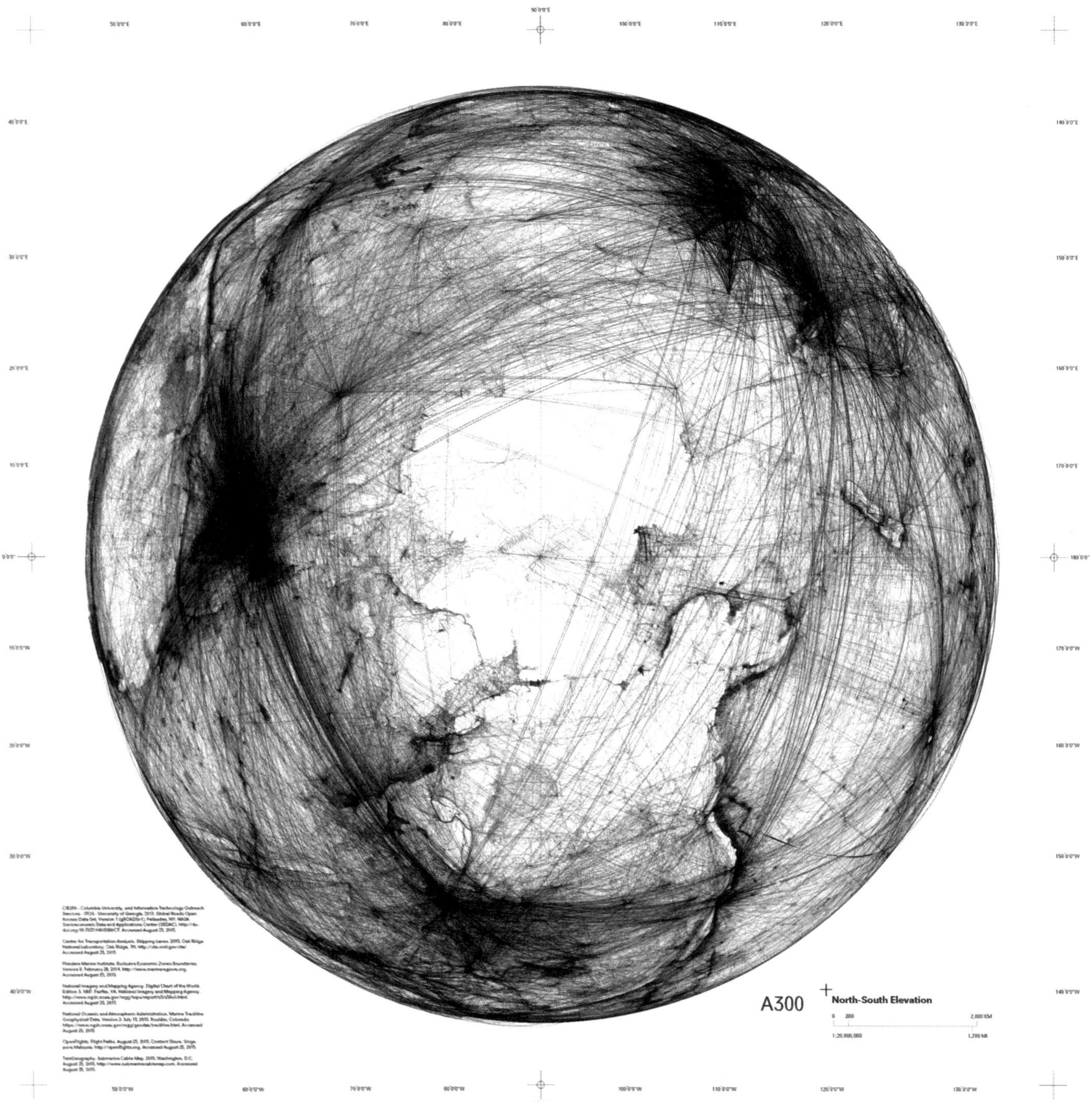

World Transport Analysis:
North – South Elevation

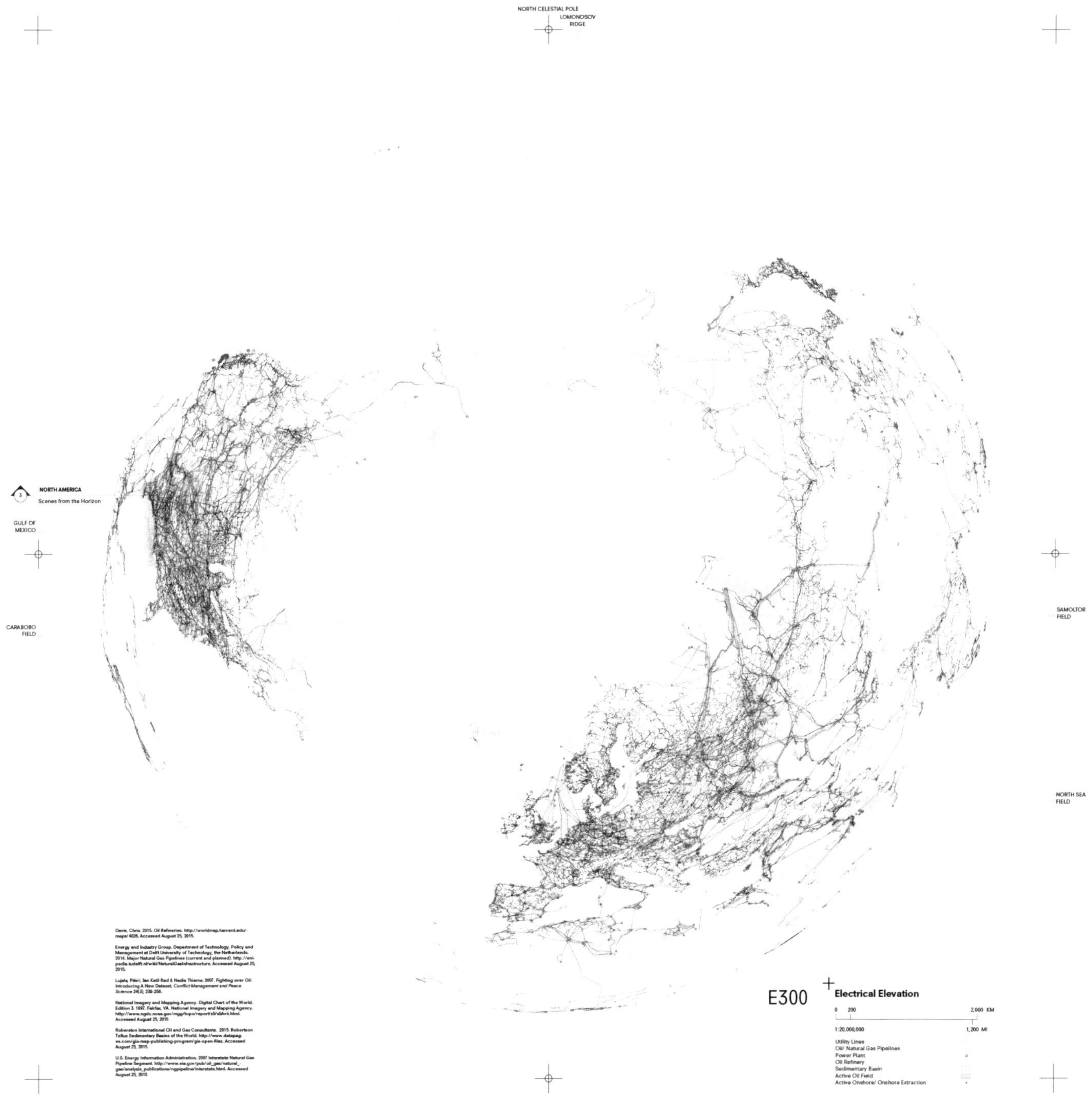

World Electrical Elevation

All images courtesy of Plan B Architecture & Urbanism.

Nora Akawi

Nora Akawi holds a Bachelor in Architecture from Bezalel Academy of Art and Design in Jerusalem and a Masters of Science in Critical, Curatorial and Conceptual Practices in Architecture from the Graduate School of Architecture, Planning and Preservation at Columbia University. Her research is focused on the role of the archive in the visualisation of collective spatial narratives and in imagining alternative spatial and political organiszation. She returned to Jerusalem in October 2011 to teach Design Studio in the Department of Architecture at the Bezalel Academy of Art and Design. Nora joined Studio-X Amman as the Curator in 2012 and is Adjunct Assistant Professor at Columbia University's Graduate School of Architecture, Planning and Preservation.

Emmanuelle Blanc

With a background in architectural studies, French based photographer Emmanuelle Blanc uses photography to express the environment, architecture and landscapes that we live in and move through. She plays with the limits of photography to bring to life architecture, emptiness and the movement of space. She has produced a series on the 'Geography of Extreme Human Occupation' in the context of the French photographic mission France(s) Territoire Liquide. Blanc was selected for the 59th 'Salon d'art contemporain de Montrouge' and has exhibited in a number of locations including Annecy, Paris and Brussels. Additionally, Blanc is sought after by major architectural firms to capture their works including that of Alvar Aalto and Jean Nouvel. Her explorations on the topics of urban planning and city heritage have also been exhibited.

Claudia Bode

Claudia Bode recently received a Master of Architecture from MIT, where she explored the tensions between architecture, landscape and politics. Currently she is a researcher at the Urban Risk Lab at MIT as well as a design studio instructor at Northeastern University in Boston. She cofounded the Kujenga Collaborative, a research and building organisation that explores strategies for (and constructs) architecture in rural Tanzania in partnership with a local nonprofit. Claudia has worked in architecture offices in Spain, Germany, the US and the Netherlands, and is currently engaged in community based design projects, operating within Lima's Urban Periphery and focusing on the role of representation in the identity of place.

Neil Brenner

Neil Brenner is Professor of Urban Theory at the Harvard Graduate School of Design, where he teaches classes on critical urban theory, urbanisation and sociospatial theory and works closely with architects, landscape architects, planners and cartographers to develop new approaches to understanding, representing and influencing contemporary worldwide urban transformations. Brenner is the author of Critique of Urbanization: Selected Essays (2016) and New State Spaces: Urban Governance and the Rescaling of Statehood (2004). He is the editor of Implosions/Explosions: Towards a Study of Planetary Urbanization (2013), and the co-editor of Cities for People, Not for Profit: Critical Urban Theory and the Right to the City (with Margit Mayer and Peter Marcuse, 2011) and Spaces of Neoliberalism (with Nik Theodore, 2002). He is currently completing several other books, including New Urban Spaces: Urban Theory and the Scale Question and Is the World Urban? Towards a Critique of Geospatial Ideology (with Nikos Katsikis). His current research, with Christian Schmid, focuses on the theorisation and investigation of emergent formations of planetary urbanisation.

Ben Butler

Ben Butler received his MFA from the School of the Art Institute of Chicago and his BA from Bowdoin College. His work has been exhibited in solo shows in New York at Coleman Burke Gallery and Plane Space, as well as at Zg Gallery in Chicago, John Davis Gallery in Hudson, New York and Davidson Galleries in Seattle, among others. He is the recipient of a Pollock-Krasner Foundation Individual Artist Grant and numerous fellowships at residency programs including the MacDowell Colony, The Bemis Center for Contemporary Art and the Ucross Foundation. To see more of Ben's Projects please go to *www.benbutlerart.com*.

Yann Defareins

Yann Defareins received a Degree from the National School of Photography in Arles in 1986 and currently lives and works in Uzes (Gard). His works ranges from commercial, report, architecture, industry and portrait based projects. He also has 20 years of teaching experience. Notions of landscape and portrait through everyday life and through times of journey (both real and imaginary) form the subject interest of DeFareins. Within this he differs in approach, technique and form. Dream, strangeness and suggestion all play a significant part in his work, where his aim is to lessen the distance between the subject and himself. 2006 saw the publication of his 'L'dée d'une femme' and in 2010 'Transversale'. He joined the photographic mission 'France(s) Territoire Liquide' in 2011.

Frédéric Delangle

Paris born photographer Frederic Delangle holds a passion for urban planning and landscape photography. Throughout the 1990s, Delangle enjoyed Paris and its suburbs through the view of his camera, a view he describes as 'marvelous'. This practice served the disciplines of architecture, landscape and urban planning, as well as institutional and advertising campaigns. 2001 saw his first trip to India, which initiated a five year project on the city of Ahmedabad. Since 2005, he has participated in a number of group and solo exhibitions. One of his most recent and well known is the co-creation of France(s) Territoire Liquide photographic mission. His contribution entitled 'PariDelhi' brings his interest in French and Indian cultures together to capture the notion of globalisation.

Design Earth

Rania Ghosn and El Hadi Jazairy are partners of DESIGN EARTH. The practice engages the geographies of technological systems to open up a range of aesthetic and political concerns for architecture and urbanism. DESIGN EARTH's work has been recognized with several awards, including the 2016 Architectural League of New York for Young Architects and the 2015 Jacques Rougerie Foundation's First Prize for "Neck of the Moon." Ghosn and Jazairy hold doctor of design degrees from Harvard University Graduate School of Design, where they were founding editors of the journal New Geographies. They are authors of the recently published Geographies of Trash (Actar, 2015), for which they received the 2014 ACSA Faculty Design Award.

Contributors

Stuart Elden

Stuart Elden is a Professor of Political Theory and Geography at the University of Warwick, within the department of Politics and International Studies. He holds an adjunct appointment as Monash Warwick Professor in the Faculty of Arts at Monash University as part of the Monash-Warwick Alliance. While Professor of Political Geography at Durham University, he held the position of Academic director of the International Boundaries Research Unit. His interests lie within the realms of philosophy, politics, geography, literature and history, seeing him contribute to these discussions through a number of published papers. In 2009 Elden published the book Terror and Territory: The Spatial Extent of Sovereignty, followed by his well known book The Birth of Territory in 2013. Elden's most recent book, Foucault's Last Decade, was published in 2016 and will be followed by more work on Foucault, Shakespeare and relations between geopolitics, earth, terrain and volume.

Olafur Eliasson

Born in 1967, Olafur Eliasson grew up in Iceland and Denmark and studied at the Royal Danish Academy of Fine Arts from 1989 to 1995. His art is driven by his interests in perception, movement, embodied experience and feelings of self. Eliasson strives to make the concerns of art relevant to society at large. Art, for him, is a crucial means for turning thinking into doing in the world. Eliasson's diverse works - in sculpture, painting, photography, film and installation - have been exhibited widely throughout the world. Not limited to the confines of the museum and gallery, his practice engages the broader public sphere through architectural projects and interventions in civic space.

Folder

Folder is a design and research practice founded by Marco Ferrari and Elisa Pasqual, and based in Milan. The studio's work spans between public and private commissions—both in the cultural and commercial domain—and the investigation of autonomous research paths. These are carried on through a diverse range of outcomes, that mostly encompasses data visualisation and the design of exhibitions, editorial and digital platforms. Folder's main research interest pivots around the understanding of contemporary technology and its effects on society, and the relation between cartography and politics. Marco Ferrari has been Creative Director of Domus magazine and is currently professor at IUAV, Venice, and ISIA, Urbino. Elisa Pasqual is a PhD candidate in Design Sciences at IUAV, Venice. Italian Limes is aproject by Folder (Marco Ferrari, Elisa Pasqual), with Delfino Sisto Legnani, Pietro Leoni, Alessandro Mason, Angelo Semeraro, Livia Shamir.

Joanne Garde-Hansen

Dr Joanne Garde-Hansen is a reader in Culture, Media and Communication, and directs the MA in Global Media and Communication at the University of Warwick. Her research and teaching focus upon media, memory, archives and heritage. This is manifest in two strands of research. The first, directly related to media, is her collaboration with television researchers on television history, heritage and memory. The second, directly related to culture and communication, is in her collaboration with geographers, water scientists and computer scientists on the relationship between culture and water, rivers, flooding and drought. She has published on (digital) media and memory, and recent books include: Media and Memory (2011), Geography and Memory (2012, with Owain Jones), Emotion Online (2013, with Kristyn Gorton), Remembering Dennis Potter (2014, with Hannah Grist) and Social Memory Technology (2016, with Karen Worcman).

Courtney A. Goode

Courtney A. Goode currently works as a Project Designer at Stoss, to which she brings her background in landscape architecture, visual media and industrial design. She holds a deep interest in urban hydrologic systems and their relationship to regional metabolism, cultural identity and human health.

Previously, she worked as a landscape architect in Melbourne, Sydney and Brussels, and has undertaken materials research in Mexico City and Bangkok. She holds a Masters in Landscape Architecture from the Harvard Graduate School of Design, and a BFA in Design with Honors from the University of Texas. While at Harvard, she was awarded the Dean's Merit Scholarship 2012-2015, the DRC Latin American Studies research grant, and worked as a design studio Teaching Assistant, CNC Milling Assistant and Research Assistant to Chris Reed and Silvia Benedito. Her work has been published in Landscape Architecture Frontiers Magazine, multiple Harvard GSD publications and exhibited in Texas, Massachusetts, Michigan and Belgium.

David Heymann

David is the young and ambitious founder of Pigeon Design Delivery. Operating across design and investigatory agendas, he works within community engagement, tertiary teaching and research. Holding a Masters in Landscape Architecture from the University of Melbourne, David takes a less traditional approach to 'landscape architecture', critically questioning its past and future trajectories. Pigeon considers a necessary shift that manifests in the materialistic rhetoric of landscape. It works under an alternate global-civic agenda, by way of the 'Neo-Infrastructural'. When not traversing global trajectories, or challenging students to push the normative, David can be found helping shape our neighbourhoods from the bottom up with Melbourne based social enterprise, CoDesign Studio.

Joyce Hsiang

Joyce Hsiang is founding principal of Plan B Architecture & Urbanism, an interdisciplinary design and research collaborative, founded in Rotterdam in 2008 and currently based in New Haven. Ongoing research projects include the design of a sustainability index to measure and manage urban development, the WorldIndexer project to model and examine the impact of development on a global scale, and the development of a parametric spatial planning methodology for the Maldives. Prior to joining the faculty at Yale, Hsiang worked at the Office for Metropolitan Architecture (OMA) in the Netherlands and Pelli Clarke Pelli in New Haven, where she led and managed the design and construction of large-scale urban projects throughout the United States, Europe, the Middle East and Asia.

Owain Jones

Owain Jones is Professor of Environmental Humanities, University of Bath Spa. Owain specialises in geographies of nature-society relations, place and landscape, community and resilience, processes of memory, nonhuman agencies, and temporalities of landscape. He is currently researching water and community issues, tidal/coastal landscapes, co-production

Extra project credits:

Cartographies of Planetary Urbanisation
Cartographies of Planetary Urbanisation is a group exhibition by three interdisciplinary research teams from ETH Zurich, ETH Future Cities Laboratory Singapore and the Urban Theory Lab at the Harvard Graduate School of Design.

Project Team Leaders
Neil Brenner, Urban Theory Lab, Harvard GSD
Christian Schmid, Urban Sociology, Dept. of Architecture, ETH Zurich
Milica Topalovic, Assistant Professor of Architecture and Territorial Planning, Dept. of Architecture, ETH Zurich

Exhibition Design
Architecture of Territory, ETH Zurich
Concept and project lead:
Milica Topalovic, Hans Hortig, Fabian Kiepenheuer.
Team: Panos a Coucopoulos, Karoline Kostka, Stefanie Krautzig, Ani Virhervaara, Lukas Wolfensberger

Graphic Design:
Goda Budvytyte

Extra project credits:

Metropolitan Processes:
Project Director
Christian Schmid

Director of Map Editing
Philippe Rekacewicz

Research Coordinator
Ozan Karaman

Research Team
Naomi Hanakata, Pascal Kallenberger, Ozan Karaman, Anne Kockelkorn, Lindsay Sawyer, Christian Schmid, Monika Streule, Rob Sullivan, Tammy Kit Ping Wong

Map Editing And Design
Dorothée Billard, Roger Conscience, Philippe Rekacewicz

Research Support
ETH Future Cities Laboratory Singapore; Dept. of Architecture, ETH Zurich.

Sources
All the maps are based on mapping sessions and interviews with experts, site visits and ethnographic field work, specific statistical data from various sources, planning documents and scientific literature.

Extra project credits:

Operational Landscapes:
Project Director
Neil Brenner

Curatorial Team
Mariano Gomez Luque, Daniel Ibañez

Research, Cartography, Video
Grga Basic, Chris Bennett, Kian Goh, Daniel Ibañez, Nikos Katsikis, Mariano Gomez Luque

Site-Specific Research and Visualisation
Dalal Musaed Al Sayer, Chris Alton, Grga Basic, Shirin Barol, Chris Bennett, Matthew Brown, Chris Buccino, Michael Chieffalo, Danika Cooper, Rob Daurio, Vineet Diwadkar, Tamer Elshayal, Leif Estrada, Ali Fard, Ghazal Jafari, Conor O'Shea, Melany Sun-Min Park, Marianne Potvin, Ana María Quiros, Roi Salgueiro, Adam Tanaka, James Whitten

Research Support
Office of the Dean, Harvard GSD; Weatherhead Center for International Affairs, Harvard University; Milton Fund, Harvard University.

of knowledge with non-humans and community, memory, flooding and resilience in a series of Arts and Humanities Research Council (AHRC) and Economic and Social Research Council (ESRC) funded projects. He has an arts background and frequently collaborates with artists and works in interdisciplinary research teams. He has published a large number of peer reviewed papers on the above subjects and has recently edited the book Geography and Memory: Identity, Place and Belonging with Joanne Garde-Hansen for the Palgrave Memory Studies Series. He is currently supervising three PhDs.

Anne Favert and Patrick Manez

Born in 1964, French photographers Anne Favert and Patrick Manez live and work in Nice, France. Since the creation of their collective some twenty-five years ago, they have been using the document image to question what covers up appearances. After several years devoted to the urban space in the form of distinct series, each one the object of a new experiment, they are currently involved in works (Metroplex, Les arpenteurs...) in which the organisation of the images between them becomes fundamental, challenging the interdependence between fiction and reality. Their idea is to develop a form of narrative that sidesteps narrative continuity and describes territories they explore, as close as possible to their own experience. Since 1994, Favert and Manez have produced a number of publications, and 2011 saw them join the collective 'France(s) Territiore Liquide'.

Bimal Mendis

Bimal Mendis conducts research on urbanisation and sustainable development. He is the recipient of the 2013 AIA Latrobe Prize for his research on the 'City of 7 Billion', which examines and models the condition of continuous urbanisation at the global scale. His research also includes the design of a 'Sustainability Index' to measure and manage urban development, which was awarded the Hines Research Grant for Advanced Sustainability in Architecture and the AIA Upjohn Research Grant. Ongoing projects include a spatial planning strategy for the Maldives and the design of a network of rural libraries in Mozambique. Prior to joining the faculty at Yale, Bimal worked at the Office for Metropolitan Architecture (OMA) in Rotterdam and Pelli Clarke Pelli Architects in New Haven, CT. Mr. Mendis received a BA and a Masters of Architecture from Yale University.

Albin Millot

Through his practice, French photographer Albin Millot tries to represent humans in space and landscapes (often urban) and to transcribe his mental images of memory and reminiscences. His photography involves both institutional and corporate assignments, in which his photographs take an aesthetic approach close to documentary photography. Personal projects explore creative alternatives to other worlds and feelings.

In 2011, he joined the project France(s) Territoire Liquide with his work on boundaries, entitled 'The Limits of France, the limits of a territory', for which he received the CNAP Fine Arts National Centre grant, via the Contemporary Documentary Photography Fund (French Culture and Communication Minister) in 2013, and an honorable mention at Bourse du Talent 2015.

Nuith Morales

Nuith Morales was born in Mexico, at a time when the price of oil dropped and the country began its current financial crisis. She is particularly interested in the spatial repercussions of social, political and environmental conflict and the capacity for intervention through manipulation of the groundplane. Her work seeks to visualise ephemeral moments and invisible forces. Nuith received a BA from Dartmouth College, where she studied Studio Art and Animation, and a Masters of Landscape Architecture from the Harvard Graduate School of Design. She worked as the main animator for The Undiscovered Country, an independent documentary about the Marshall Islands, and hopes to apply similar research and film sensibilities to landscape. She is the recipient of various grants, including the Alfred K. Priest Fellowship and research funding from the Dickey Center for International Understanding. Nuith is currently a landscape designer at Sasaki Associates.

Clara Oloriz

Clara Olóriz Sanjuán is a PhD architect, tutor and practising architect. She works as design director at Groundlab, specialised in the design of public spaces and masterplans from a landscape and urban perspective in various international contexts. Currently, she teaches at the AA Landscape Urbanism masters programme. She also co-directs the AA Visiting School 'Computing Topos' in Bilbao and the AA Research Cluster 'Urban Prototypes.' She has published extensively and lectured in several professional and academic venues in Venice, Leeds, Cambridge, Amsterdam, Uppsala, Lausanne, Surat, London, Mexico, Pamplona, Porto or Bilbao.

Rene Peralta

A native of Tijuana, Mexico Rene Peralta has taught and practiced architecture in the border region from Tijuana to Los Angeles. His academic training in architecture began in San Diego and later in London at the Architectural Association, where he studied with Jeffrey Kipnis and Bahram Shirdel from 1995-96. After the AA, Peralta resettled in Tijuana/San Diego and in the year 2000 opened his own practice, an 'alternative' practice operating in one of the most hectic and volatile regions of North America.

It is between these paradoxical borderlands that Peralta finds inspiration to research the urban environment and architectural affinities within the region, as well as producing work (academic and professional) related to many contemporary urban issues in Latin America. Currently, he directs the Landscape Urbanism graduate program at Woodbury University San Diego, and has a practice in the city of Tijuana, where he lives. Over the last 16 years Peralta has maintained a practice involved in architectural and urban research as well as being an active participant in academic activities on both sides of the border.

Peralta's current interests are to continue to pursue architectural/urban research beyond border phenomena, and to promote and share the experience and work realised in the last 16 years as it pertains to this region and the type of practice engendered by these global/local conditions. He is interested in academic research on global and contested urbanism and landscapes of the liminal border condition he finds himself in.

Jose Alfredo Ramirez

Jose Alfredo Ramirez is an architect co-founder and director of Groundlab and Director of the Landscape Urbanism MArch/MSc Graduate Programme at the Architectural Association. Jose Alfredo has worked and developed projects at the junction of architecture, landscape and urbanism in a variety of contexts such as China,

Mexico, Spain, Russia, Chile among others. He concentrates mainly in large scale development of public spaces like the Olympic Master Plan for London 2012 and recently the redevelopment of 12 km of Santiago de Chile's main avenue, Alameda/Providencia into an integral transport and urban corridor. Other projects, includes the redevelop Sokolniki Park, the biggest park in Moscow, the ongoing development for a Master Plan to relocate a Train Station in the city of Innichen, Italy and the built complex for the International Horticultural Exhibition opened in Xian, China.

Jose Alfredo is also the Director of the AA Visiting School In Mexico City, and has published a number of articles and a book 'Critical Territories:' as well as given workshops and lectured on the topic of Landscape Urbanism and the work of Groundlab worldwide.

Brent D. Ryan

Brent Ryan is Associate Professor of Urban Design and Public Policy and Head of the City Design and Development Group at MIT. His work examines the aesthetics and practice of contemporary urban design, particularly in post-industrial cities and neighborhoods. He is author of two books: Plural Urbanism, which will be published by MIT Press in 2017, and Design After Decline: How America rebuilds shrinking cities, which was selected by Planetizen as one of its ten best urban planning books of 2012. Prior to joining MIT, Ryan taught at the Harvard Graduate School of Design and the University of Illinois at Chicago, where he was also Co-Director of the City Design Center. Ryan holds a Bachelor of Science in biology from Yale University, a Masters of Architecture from Columbia University and a PhD in urban design and planning from MIT.

Saskia Sassen

Saskia Sassen is the Robert S. Lynd Professor of Sociology and chairs the Committee on Global Thought, Columbia University. She is a student of cities, immigration and states in the world economy, with inequality, gendering and digitisation three key variables running though her work. She is the author of eight books and the editor or co-editor of three books, which have been translated into over 20 languages.

Her latest book is Expulsions: Brutality and Complexity in the Global Economy (Harvard University Press/Belknap 2014). It launches a fourth major research project in her academic career. The organising thesis is that our global modernity is marked by systemic expulsions of all sorts: we are beyond simply more inequality, more poverty, more refugees in the global south, and so on. And it is often our complex intermediary processes, requiring talent and knowledge, which are facilitating such expulsions.

Kris Scheerlinck

Kris Scheerlinck is Associate Professor in Architecture and Urban Projects at KU Leuven. He initially trained as an Architect at the School of Architecture, Sint-Lucas, Ghent, specialising in Spatial Planning (University of Ghent/KU Leuven) and in Urban Design (UPC Barcelona). He holds a PhD in Architecture and Urban Projects from UPC/URL (Barcelona, Spain), supervised by Manuel de Solà-Morales and Amador Ferrer. For more than 15 years, he ran his own design practice in Ghent, Barcelona and New York, working in the research and design of architecture, landscape and urban projects. He coordinated and taught design studios and theoretical courses in Architecture and Urban Design Programs at various institutions and universities in New York, Barcelona, Bratislava, Melbourne, Valparaiso, Cordoba, Guayaquil, Cuenca, Ghent and Brussels. He is currently Vice-Dean for International Affairs at the Faculty of Architecture of KU Leuven. He is Head of the Research Group 'Urban Projects, Collective Spaces and Local Identities' at the Department of Architecture. He directs an international research project on depth configurations in urban projects, called 'Streetscape Territories' and promotes related PhD projects. His expertise is on the analysis of public-private gradients in urban landscapes and their related models of accessibility, permeability and proximity and pronounces a critical discourse on territorial boundary delimitation in real-life projects.

Christian Schmid

Christian Schmid is a geographer, sociologist and urban researcher. He is Titular Professor of Sociology at the Department of Architecture, ETH Zurich and researcher at ETH Studio Basel/Contemporary City Institute. Since 1980, Schmid has been active as video activist, organiser of cultural events and urban researcher. In 1991 he was cofounder of the International Network for Urban Research and Action (INURA). Schmid has authored, co-authored and co-edited numerous publications on theories of the urban and of space, on Henri Lefebvre, on territorial urban development and on the comparative analysis of urbanisation. He currently works together with Neil Brenner on the theorisation and investigation of emergent formations of planetary urbanisation. In the framework of the ETH Future Cities Laboratory Singapore he leads a project on the comparison of urbanisation processes in the urban areas of Tokyo, Hong Kong/Shenzhen/Dongguan, Kolkata, Istanbul, Lagos, Paris, Mexico City and Los Angeles.

Cooking Sections

Cooking Sections (Daniel Fernández Pascual & Alon Schwabe) is a duo of spatial practitioners based out of London. It was born to explore the systems that organize the WORLD through FOOD. Using installation, performance, mapping and video, their research-based practice explores the overlapping boundaries between visual arts, architecture and geopolitics. Cooking Sections was part of the exhibition at the U.S. Pavilion, 2014 Venice Architecture Biennale. Their work has also been exhibited at the Neue Nationalgalerie Berlin; Storefront for Art & Architecture New York; dOCUMENTA(13); Peggy Guggenheim Collection; CA2M; the Bartlett; ETSAM; TEDx Talks Madrid; Fiorucci Art Trust London; ACC Weimar; SOS 4.8; HKW Berlin; 2014 Biennale INTERIEUR Kortrijk; and have been 2014 residents in The Politics of Food at Delfina Foundation, London.

Milica Topalovic

Milica Topalovic is Assistant Professor of Architecture & Territorial Planning at the Swiss Federal Institute of Technology ETH Zurich. She held a research professorship at the ETH Future Cities Laboratory in Singapore from 2011-15, and was head of research at the ETH Studio Basel Contemporary City Institute from 2006-11. Her research and teaching focuses on territorial urbanisation, in particular the relations between cities and their hinterlands.

She graduated with distinction from the Faculty of Architecture in Belgrade and received a Masters degree from the Dutch Berlage Institute with a thesis on Belgrade's postsocialist urban transformation.

With ETH Studio Basel she authored and edited Belgrade Formal/Informal: A Research on Urban

Extra project credits:

Hinterland: Singapore and Urbanisms Beyond the Border (p 98)

Project Director
Milica Topaloalovic

Research and Visualisation
Sand: Hans Hortig; Water: Architecture of Territory and Benjamin Leclair-Paquet; Food: Marcel Jaeggi; Labour: Ahmed Belkhodja, Saskja Odermatt; Oil: Lino Moser; Cross-Border Metropolitan Region Singapore, Johor, Riau: Karoline Kostka; Hinterland Typology Drawings: Ani Virhervaara, Bek Tai Keng

Photographs
Bas Princen

Teaching Team (2011-2015)
Hans Hortig, Marcel Jaeggi, Martin Knuesel, Stefanie Krautzig

Student Researchers (2011-2015)
Ahmed Belkhodja, Desiree Damport, Pascal Deschenaux, Martin Garcia, Giulia Luraschi, Livio De Maria, Lino Moser, Magnus Nickl, Saskja Odermatt, Myriam Perret, Gabriela Schär, Stephanie Schenk, Caroline Schillinger, Karl Wruck, Simon Zemp

Exhibition Design
Architecture of Territory.
Concept and Project Lead:
Milica Topalovic, Hans Hortig, Fabian Kiepenheuer.
Team: Panos a Coucopoulos, Stefanie Krautzig, Lukas Wolfensberger.
Graphic design: Goda Budvytyte

Research Support
ETH Future Cities Laboratory Singapore, Dept. of Architecture, ETH Zurich 2011–2015.

Extra image credits:

Christian Schmid
Metropolitan Processes (p 94)
Metropolitan Processes:
Los Angeles: Work in progress, November 2015. Urban Sociology, ETH Future Cities Laboratory Singapore: Planetary Urbanization in Comparative Perspective. Ethnographic fieldwork and mapping: Ozan Karaman, Christian Schmid, Rob Sullivan. Map design and editing: Philippe Rekacewicz

Metropolitan Processes: Hong Kong, Shenzhen, Dongguan: Work in progress, November 2015. Urban Sociology, ETH Future Cities Laboratory Singapore: Planetary Urbanization in Comparative Perspective. Ethnographic fieldwork and mapping: Tammy Kit Ping Wong. Map design and editing: Philippe Rekacewicz

Neil Brenner
Operational Landscapes (p 96)
Artic:
Grga Basic, Urban Theory Lab Harvard GSD

Amazon:
Ali Fard, Daniel Ibanez and others, Urban Theory Lab Harvard GSD

Atmosphere:
Chris Bennett, Urban Theory Lab Harvard GSD

Milica Topalovic
Hinterland: Singapore and Urbanisms Beyond the Border (p 98)
Hinterland Typologies:
Work in progress, December 2015. Assistant Professor of Architecture and Territorial Planning, ETH Zurich and ETH Future Cities Laboratory Singapore: Hinterland, Singapore Beyond the Border. Research: Architecture of Territory 2011-ongoing. Map drawing: Ani Vihervaara 2015

Cross-Border Metropolitan Region Singapore, Johor, Riau Archipelago: Work in progress, December 2015. Assistant Professor of Architecture and Territorial Planning, ETH Zurich and ETH Future Cities Laboratory Singapore: Hinterland, Singapore Beyond the Border. Research: Architecture of Territory 2011-2015. Map research, design and mapping: Karoline Kostka 2015

Cartographies of Planetary Urbanisation
Exhibition Photography by Bas Princen

Transformation showing informality in the global north, and The Inevitable Specificity of Cities on territory, power and difference in cities and urban regions such as Hong Kong, Casablanca and the Nile Valley. She is currently working on the forthcoming book Hinterland: Singapore Beyond the Border, and conducting research and design studios on European Countryside.

Emilie Vialet

The major focus of Emilie Vialet's practice is to investigate those places where nature is used to fill or cover the scars of a brutal change. She graduated from the Fine Arts School in 2003, and completed her studies in photography at the National School Louis Lumière in 2006, writing a thesis on the theme of contemporary landscapes. She realised several series on functional spaces offering neither space for walking nor contemplation (such as roundabouts, the borders of motorway or nuclear testing areas in France). In 2011, she joined the mission "France(s) Liquids territories" in which she participates by photographing a territory totally domesticated by man: the Landes (France).

In 2015, her current and ongoing project 'The eternal' has been awarded the grant for photographic creation 'Regards without Limits/ Blicke ohne Grenzen'. The project resulted in a series of exhibitions through various countries of the Greater Region (Belgium, Germany, Luxembourg and France). She is represented by Schumm-Braunstein Gallery, Paris and Arlesian Countertops of Young Photography Gallery, Arles.

Alberto Villanueva

Alberto Villanueva is a Spanish architect. He completed his Masters of Architecture and a MA in Environment Design at Ravensbourne with a distinction, and has a background generating content in digital communication and interactive aspects. Alberto has developed projects and collaborations with international architecture firms. He researches the possibilities of 3D printers and new materials, with emphasis in the colonisation of Mars, as a solution to generate architectures in extreme environments.

Currently he is tutoring in Critical Practice and the Coordinator of the Mentoring Programme for the Postgraduate Courses and Sessional Lecturer in Contextual Studies at Ravensbourne (London). Alberto is director and founder of IDEA architecture office based in London with collaborators in Madrid and New York, and has been noted by The Royal Academy of Arts and featured in publications like Dezeen, designboom, Archdaily, The Spaces and DesignCurial.

Terri Warpinski

From her home base in Eugene, Oregon, artist/ photographer Terri Warpinski travels the world in her creative practice. Terri is a Professor of Art at the University of Oregon and was a Fulbright Scholar in Israel in 2000-2001. In 2014 she was awarded an Individual Artist Fellowship, and in 2013 and 2016 she was awarded Career Opportunity Grants, all through the Ford Family Foundation and Oregon Arts Commission. Her work has been shown internationally in more than a hundred exhibitions, at such venues as the Pingyao International Festival of Photography in China, the US Embassy in Jerusalem, Houston International Fotofest, the Center for Photography in Woodstock, New York, the University of the Arts in Philadelphia and Camerawork in San Francisco. In 2015 she completed a collaboration entitled Liminal Matter, addressing the US-Mexican borderlands. This limited edition set has been added to the special collections of the libraries of the University of California Berkeley, the University of Washington, Texas State University San Marcos and Stanford University. Her solo exhibition Surface Tension opened in 2014 in Fort Collins, Colorado, and will travel through 2017 to venues in Nebraska, Illinois, New Mexico, New York, Pennsylvania, Arizona and Ohio.

Paul Wombell

French born Paul Wombell is an independent curator and writer on photography currently based in London. His interests lie in photography, machines and what it means to be human. Wombell has previously directed a number of galleries including Impressions Gallery and The Photographers Gallery. He has curated a number of exhibitions including international photography festivals and individual exhibitions. Additionally he has edited nine books on photography. Since 2011, Wombell has been the artistic director of the photographic mission, France(s) Territoire Liquide. This saw the direction of over 43 photographers, producing 41 projects and 500 photographs, that together delve into the idea of France as a liquid territory.

Yujun Yin

Yujun Yin is co-founder of Projective Architecture Office (PAO). He received his Masters of Architecture and Masters of Landscape Architecture from Harvard University Graduate School of Design. He was a senior researcher at Harvard University and received the Dean Research Funding. His research and practice focus on architecture design as a spatial means to weave the urban environment and create active and vibrant public life. Project highlights include Shenzhen Bay B-Tec (Bio-Technical-City), Buenos Aires National Art Gallery, Shenzhen Haina Baichuan Tower and Shenzhen Xiasha Bay urban design. He has participated in the 2005, 2007, 2009, 2011, 2013 and 2015 SZ/HK Bi-city Biennale of Urbanism/ Architecture and the 2011 Venice Biennale. He also co-curated the affordable housing competition exhibition 'Livable City Among Others' in 2011. His work was part of the Architecture China 100 exhibition in Reiss-Engelhorn-Museen in 2012. His critical writing has been published in Harvard Platform, DOMUS, Time Architecture and Urban Architecture.

mark your territory
#kerbcomp

Kerb's Instagram followers were given the opportunity to explore and consider how the notion of territory plays out in their local landscape through photography. These images here were seen to be the most provocative submissions relating to our theme.

Kerb would like to say thankyou to everyone who submitted an entry, and to congratulate our nine winners,

Sebastián Betancur
Struan Brown
Heather Chapman
Xujie Fang
James Kellock
Monica Naranjo
Svetlana Pavkovic
Angelica Rodriguez
Ceren Sozer

Advertising and Sponsorship

The **Kerb** production team and the RMIT Landscape Architecture program would like to thank our sponsors for their generous financial support toward this not-for-profit publication.

••

RMIT Architecture and Design

••

PATRON

Taylor Cullity Lethlean

T.C.L

LANDSCAPE ARCHITECTURE
URBAN DESIGN

••

BENEFACTORS

OCULUS

••

FRIENDS

Sue Barnsley Design

Collie Pty Ltd